Who Gets Your Stuff When You Die

By Leigh Hilton

Book Design by Lori Henderson of Concept2Creation

Cover Photo by Suade Bejtović

Leigh
Hilton
P.L.L.C.

About the Author

Leigh Hilton is an Accredited Estate Planner* who has guided more than 6,000 families through the process of protecting their assets from divorce, creditors, lawsuits, and predators.

She has also helped more than 1,500 families implement estate plans after the death or incapacity of a loved one.

Leigh has more than 26 years of legal experience in the practice areas of estate planning and probate. She is the author of *Who Gets Your Stuff When You Die?* and a frequent speaker to various organizations and groups. She's given more than 400 speeches during her career.

Whether your estate is large or small, simple or complex, Leigh and her team would welcome the opportunity to meet you and discuss your estate planning needs. She can also assist with special needs, Medicaid, and VA benefits.

Leigh was born in Dallas and grew up in Denton, Texas. She attended the University of North Texas, where she earned a Bachelor of Science degree and graduated with honors in 1989. She earned her law degree at the South Texas College of Law, where she graduated Summa Cum Laude in 1992. She's been married for 32 years and is the proud mother of two boys.

Leigh Hilton is proud to provide legal counsel rooted in Christian values.

Leigh Hilton, PLLC

www.leighhilton.net

940-387-8800

First Published in 2017 by Leigh Hilton P.L.L.C

Copyright 2020 Leigh Hilton

ISBN:10:XXXXXXXXXXX

Legal Disclaimer

No part of this publication may be reproduced or transmitted in any form or by any means, mechanical or electronic, including photocopying or recording, or by any information storage and retrieval system, or transmitted by email without permission in writing from the author.

While all attempts have been made to verify the information provided in this publication, neither the author nor the publisher assumes any responsibility for errors, omissions, or contrary interpretations of the subject matter herein.

This book is for educational purposes only. This book is based upon the personal experiences of the Author. No portion of this book is intended to provide legal, financial or professional advice. The information contained herein is not a substitute or replacement for the services of qualified professionals, legal, financial and insurance experts.

The Author, its publisher, agents, servants, contractors, employees and representatives will, under no circumstances, be liable for any special or consequential damages that result from the use of, or any attempt to use, the information contained herein. You are solely responsible and accountable for any actions, decisions and results by your use of the information contained herein. You agree not to attempt to hold us liable for any such decision, actions, or results, at any time, under any circumstances.

Adherence to all applicable laws and regulations, including international, federal, state and local governing professional licensing, business practices, advertising, and all other aspects of doing business in the US, Canada or any other jurisdiction is the sole responsibility of the purchaser or reader.

Any perceived slight of any individual or organization is purely unintentional.

Author's Notes

Thank you for downloading my book.

To learn more about the Author and her company click on any of the following links:

Leigh Hilton P.L.L.C website (www.leighhilton.net)

Leigh Hilton on Facebook (www.facebook.com/dentonestateplanninglawyer)

Leigh Hilton on Youtube (www.youtube.com/user/dentonattorney)

Leigh Hilton on LinkedIn (www.linkedin.com/in/leighhilton)

Leigh Hilton on Twitter (www.twitter.com/LeighHiltonatty)

After you have read this book, please provide a review on Amazon so that I can make future versions even better. Your reviews are greatly appreciated

Bonus Available Here!

Go to https://View.WhoGetsYourStuffWhenYouDie.com and enter your email then press Let Me View It.

You'll receive these free bonuses: access to view the "WHO gets your STUFF when YOU DIE?" seminar

And Free Membership to our Newsletter

Do it today! Offer only good for a limited time!

Thank you!

Table of Contents

———— ∞ ————

Table of Contents continued

Endorsements by Professionals

"Death and financial matters are two topics that many people tend to shy away from. Sometimes that is due to the emotional stress brought on by these subjects, while other times it is the overwhelming amount of information that can be difficult to wade through. Fortunately, we are blessed to have Leigh Hilton here in North Texas to help simplify these matters. Her writing style softens the hard edges of these topics, while her charming personality calms her clients and seminar attendees as she shares her vast estate planning knowledge and expertise. Leigh is simply one of the best attorneys that I've come across who is exceptional at helping her clients." – **Matt Slaton,** Financial Planner, Insight Financial Group

"Leigh Hilton has taken a complicated subject and broken it down so that it is easy to digest. It is written in plain English so everyone can better understand the subject matter. Most people think estate planning is just for the wealthy. After reading this book it becomes clear that everyone should have a well-thought-out estate plan. I will make this required reading for my agents and I will give copies to my clients." ---

Ray Croff, CLU, ChFC, CAP, RFC, CEPA, Managing Partner, Turtle Creek Financial Group

"Leigh is the authority in Elder Law and Estate Planning in North Texas. She is extremely gifted in simplifying what can be a complex and confronting subject for most families. This is a must-read for everyone concerned with protecting their legacy." --- **Wesley Pingelton**, CFP®, CFA, FullCircle Wealth

"As in her other publications, Leigh does not disappoint. Estate Planning can be daunting, and Leigh walks you through real-life scenarios that are invaluable to understand and helpful in avoiding procrastination on the inevitable we all face. Leigh relates real-life scenarios and makes them easy to understand and apply. We are lucky to have her as an outsourced strategic partner and recommend everyone take the time to read this. I promise there is something in it for everyone to use." -- **Wayne Holt,** Financial Planner, Insight Financial Group

"Like many of my friends, I am navigating the challenges of loving my mom while she deals with the challenges of aging. Her biggest fear in this process centers around her 'stuff.' It is her desire to ensure that her children will not fight over it, and that it can be put to good use to help the people she loves. Leigh Hilton has crafted a great book to help parents with kids, and kids with parents to address those issues before it is too late. I strongly encourage you to take advantage of Leigh's 14 secrets to jump-start a conversation and proactively solve issues." -- **Glenn Gutek**, Certified Practice Advisor, Atticus Inc.

"Whether you are a Gen X, Gen Y, or Baby Boomer like myself with aging parents, you will find this book extremely helpful in understanding the different estate planning strategies that can provide so many benefits to your family. Leigh shares many case stories throughout the book and makes difficult legal terms and concepts for any layperson easy to understand. If you are in any way concerned about how to provide and protect your family assets, you owe it to yourself to read this book." -- **Juan C. Bustamante**, Major and Planned Giving Officer, Good Samaritan Foundation

"This book is an excellent description of the overall needs of an individual or family relative to their financial, medical, or legal needs. The details provide a route that individuals need to increase their personal security in life." -- **Dr. Derrell W. Bulls**, Retired Faculty Ombudsman, Texas Woman's University

"Written in an easy and direct style with stories that are both real and relatable, in her book *Who Gets Your Stuff When You Die?* Leigh Hilton provides everyone access to understanding estate planning issues. Presented in concise chapters that end with 'takeaways' for consideration on each subject, Leigh describes and turns estate planning terminology into phrases that are educational, practical, and applicable. If you have an interest in directing where your 'stuff' goes when you die, I see this book as an invaluable tool for you, your estate, and your family. Having been in similar situations to what Leigh describes, I can attest to how important it is to understand estate planning before you really need it. I suggest this book to my staff, fellow attorneys, clients, and family as highly recommended reading, timely for each of us." -- **Charla H. Bradshaw**, Attorney and Managing Shareholder, KoonsFuller, Family Law P.C.

"Benjamin Franklin said there are only two things certain in life: death and taxes. As a CPA, I can certainly attest to one of these certainties. Thankfully, we have attorneys like Leigh Hilton who are willing to walk us through the other certainty. In *Who Gets Your Stuff When You Die?* Leigh has taken a subject many do not want to address and made it extremely easy to read and digest. Her decades of experience in this area have resulted in a book that will be invaluable to everyone, regardless of age or financial status. She has included interesting real-life stories as well as end-of-chapter 'takeaways' that concisely summarize each chapter. Without a doubt, I highly recommend this book not only to others, but to my clients as well." -- **Jan Burns Springer, CPA**, Partner, Howe & Springer, P.C.

"*Who Gets Your Stuff When You Die?* is an easy-to-follow road map for

dealing with an event in one's life that cannot be avoided. The practical reason for this type of planning is easy to see. The process will be done. It will be done with someone's direction. Individuals can now see that much of the work can be done prior to their death at a controllable cost, with detailed input. This is in sharp contrast to the events that can occur *after* death without proper planning. It simply is easier, and more accurately reflects the wishes of the parties." -- **Mark J. Merki, CPA, CGMA**

Why I Am Writing About This Stuff

I have been an attorney for nearly three decades. During this time, I have had the privilege of helping over six thousand families create, modify, and implement their estate plans. We talk through best- and worst-case scenarios. And we walk through a variety of options to meet their unique family situations.

I have also helped over 300 families implement the plans that I have designed after their loved ones pass away, and helped over 1200 clients implement the plans that other attorneys have designed.

As you may imagine, I have seen estate plans work extremely well— and I have seen things go completely haywire through lack of planning and bitter feuding.

That is why I am writing this book. I know firsthand how overwhelming estate planning can be for clients and their families. And without an attorney who knows his or her stuff, well, *your stuff* could be in jeopardy.

I don't want to see that happen to anyone, whether you are my client or not! My hope is that this book will help you think clearly through practical, inevitable topics we must all consider sooner or later.

Families that are willing to do their research, hire professional help, and openly discuss difficult topics are the ones who worry less because they leave less to worry about. While this book does not cover every single detail of estate planning (that would kill too many trees!), it does cover a great many scenarios I have personally handled and helped my clients effectively work through.

My sincere hope is that it helps you make the best possible plan for yourself and your family.

Leigh Hilton

www.leighhilton.net

When Everything Works as It Should

Jim and Joan (not their real names) came in to see me several years ago. Jim's father had recently passed away and he had a Living Trust. Jim was very pleased at how easy that made it for him and his brothers. The Living Trust specified the recipients of the assets and how those assets were to be managed. This trust made it possible for Jim to take over the trust and divide the assets among himself and his brothers, as his father had wished, without having to go to court.

Jim and Joan wanted things to go as smoothly for their own family as it had in Jim's father's situation. They wanted to make sure that when one of them passed away, the surviving spouse would be taken care of. Whatever remained after the survivor's death would then be divided equally among their four children. One problem, however: Jim and Joan did not like one of their sons-in-law. They were frustrated over how he treated their daughter. They also believed that he would influence her to spend money unwisely. Another child was in a business that made him vulnerable to getting sued. The youngest child was not good with money. They thought about putting the eldest child in charge of the youngest child's money. I spoke with them about the tension that this could cause between the children.

I then designed a trust for them that Jim and Joan controlled during their lifetimes. If either of them passed away or became incompetent, the other one would remain in charge. They wanted to make sure that the remaining assets were given to their children and that the surviving spouse could not give their assets to a new spouse, pick a favorite child, or leave the assets to a random charity. Jim and Joan decided to use a corporate trustee to manage the trust after they both passed away. They realized that putting one child in charge of another child's money could cause conflict. The trust also protected the children's inheritance from divorce, creditors, and lawsuits. It made sure that, in the event of a child's death, the assets of that child would go to the grandchildren. They were excited to have their family so well protected. It gave them great peace of mind.

Several years later, Jim died and Joan became the manager of the trust. In time, when Joan married again, she came in to have a new trust prepared for her and her new husband. That meeting went very smoothly, because there was no need to discuss the assets that had previously belonged to Jim. They were already in a trust that would be managed by Joan during her life and on her death would benefit Jim and Joan's children. Without this trust being in place, the conversation would have been very different.

Most wills are what we call "I love you" wills. These wills shortsightedly leave everything to the spouse. That can create issues, especially in the case of stepparents. On more than one occasion a stepmother has promised to leave the assets to her stepchildren, but later came to me and said, "I know that everything was left to me with the understanding that I would leave it to his children, but he didn't realize what jerks they were going to be after he was gone." I have also heard, "If he knew how they were acting, he would want me to disinherit them."

Many years later, when Joan passed away, her daughter was in the middle of a divorce. One of her sons had filed bankruptcy. Another son was disabled and receiving Medicaid. They were grateful that their parents had set up the trust for their benefit that protected them. If the trust had not been set up properly, all three of those children would have lost some or all of what they inherited. Only the fourth child would have gone unscathed. The daughter who was divorcing her husband would have had the assets she inherited considered when dividing the community property. Since the daughter did not own the trust assets outright, she was able to retain the benefit of them. The judge considered only those assets owned mutually by the couple in fairly dividing their community property. Joan's son, who was in the middle of a bankruptcy, did not have his trust fund assets included in the assets that the bankruptcy judge would be dividing. Without the trust, his entire inheritance would have been paid to his creditors. Joan's son who was on

Medicaid would have lost his Medicaid benefits due to having excess assets. He would have been taken off of Medicaid until after he had spent everything that he inherited. Because the trust specified that it could be used only for expenditures not covered by Medicare/Medicaid, he was able to continue receiving that benefit while having some discretionary funds available to cover other costs of living and care for his special needs. The foresight of Joan, Jim, and a well-crafted trust ensured that their legacy was used in the manner they intended. That is how estate planning should work.

Chapter One

Distributing Your Stuff

The words "wealth" and "estate" often bring to mind million-dollar mansions with beautiful rolling lawns, swimming pool waterfalls, and five-car garages. Nice images, but not what we are talking about in this chapter.

Estate planning is simply about deciding what will be done with "your stuff" in the event of your death or disability. Simple as that.

Your wealth transfer strategy needs to be tailored to your assets and your family situations. When clients first come to talk about planning, I ask *lots* of questions. I want to know about each child, each grandchild, and any other beneficiaries. I want to know more than just how many there are and their names. I want to know all about them. What do they do for a living? Are they good at handling money and other responsibilities? Will they be responsible if they inherit a large sum money? Then I will ask the same questions regarding their spouses. I will also ask if anyone in the family has a disability. These are not idle questions. I am looking for issues that need to be addressed in the will or trust, which is then customized to the unique family situation. By getting to know the family, I can make sure that the client's family is taken care of in the manner that the client chooses.

Let's Get Really Real

Now, in order to create the best estate plan for my clients, I tell them: "I need to know about your real family. Not the family you wish you had or the family you think others have because of what they post on Facebook."

Sometimes when I meet with a family, they are embarrassed that there is some dysfunction in their family. I think we need to come up with a new label for dysfunctional -- like *normal* or *usual* or *common*. Most people I meet with have some dysfunction in their family. Some of them are lucky enough to have to go out to cousins before we see dysfunction, but for a lot of us the dysfunction is closer to home.

Several years ago, I met a lady who told me about her fairy-tale son. He was the perfect son who called her often and sent her flowers. I should have known he was too good to be true. We prepared a plan that put him in charge of her medically and financially if she were ever to become incompetent.

A few years later, she was diagnosed with dementia and I got to meet her *real* son. They hadn't spoken in years and did not have a good relationship.

If she had told me about her real son and their strained relationship, we could have designed a plan to ensure one of her good friends was able to take charge of her medical and financial decisions if the need ever arose. Instead, she and her son ended up in a lengthy court battle for control of the assets.

Question Everything

To avoid circumstances like the one above, I ask my clients lots of questions. I am not trying to be nosy. I am listening for red flags and reassurances. That is why I want to know about each child, each grandchild and any other beneficiaries. Here are a few questions I typically ask:

- What does he/she do for a living?
- Are they good at handling money and other responsibilities?
- Will they be responsible if they inherit a large sum money?

Then I will ask the same questions regarding their spouses. I will also ask if anyone in the family has a disability. Like I said, these are not idle questions. I am looking for issues that need to be addressed as we create each client's will or trust.

I have been doing this for enough years that I know how to spot possible problems—and how to work through those with each client. The will or trust is then customized to each family's situation. By getting to know my clients and their families, I can make sure they are taken care of in the exact manner they desire.

Should You Create a Will or a Trust?

Given that both wills and trusts are instruments designed to specify who gets your stuff when you die, how do you decide which to use? Great question! We'll dig into this more later, but for now here is a quick rundown of the key differences:

- Wills are usually simpler and less expensive for the individual, but more cumbersome and expensive for heirs. In other words, wills are cheaper in the short run and more expensive in the long run. They also do not cover the possibility of incapacity, nor do they protect sensitive information you may wish to keep private.

- Trusts are usually more complex and therefore may cost more upfront. That is because they often result in less work and less expense for the beneficiaries. Trusts also cover circumstances such as disability and incapacity, whether temporary or permanent. And they may be kept private.

Your particular circumstances and concerns should be considered when choosing a will or trust. You should discuss both options with your estate planning attorney, who will know the right choice for your family's needs.

Customize, Customize, Customize

It is important to customize your estate plan to your particular assets. For example, if you have a family business, then the plan needs to spell out what will happen to that business:

- Will the business be sold and the proceeds divided?
- How will the money be distributed?
- Who will take care of all the necessary business related to the sale, including what price to ask and ultimately accept?
- If the business is to continue to be owned by one or more heirs, specific ownership rights and privileges must be addressed.

Out-of-state property also requires additional planning to avoid probate in the other state. Thoughtful customization on the front end can save both time and money down the road.

You also have choices as to how an asset may be given to a successor. The gift may be given outright, with no strings attached, or with conditions.

For instance, someone may specify that their estate be divided between their living children, except for one who is disabled. That child's portion would go into a supplemental-needs trust established for that child.

Or, a person may be given use of a property during his or her lifetime, after which the property would go to a specific other owner.

The donor may even specify that the property must never be used for a specific reason, such as a gambling establishment. If such use were proven, the property would revert to a specific charity. Such a condition would be unusual, but not all wills or trusts are the same. Remember, a will or trust can be customized according to your exact wishes.

Trusts Can Be Flexible

As I prepare estate plans for each of my clients, I also add language to cover things that could change in the future.

For example, I always include a standby supplemental-needs trust in all the estate plans I draft. This is to protect beneficiaries if they later become disabled and have a need for government benefits.

I also include a provision for a trust protector. This allows the trust or will to adapt to circumstances we can't predict—without requiring court involvement. Changes can be made with the help of an attorney. The trust protector can also correct errors in the trust or will. Here are a few more benefits of a trust:

- *Trusts can easily adapt if you move to another state.* (There are fewer differences in trust laws and their interpretation from state to state.)

- *Trusts can be more flexible than wills.* They are actually contracts and therefore can contain any specifics a person's situation requires.

- *Trusts can protect a family's privacy.* The details of a trust are not public record, while the contents of a will are. If, for example, there is a need to have someone else administer the funds when there is a beneficiary issue (such as drug addiction or cognitive disability), this need not be made public knowledge. The additional privacy may also protect beneficiaries from others who may be likely to take advantage of them.

- *A trustee can carry on with necessary business affairs.* The trust will specify how incapacity would be determined. Our trusts usually call for the signatures of two physicians on a document that states the person who created the trust is unable to carry out his or her affairs. Authority would then transfer to the next trustee named in the trust. No court action would be necessary. If the person recovers, or is determined to have been competent all along, a similar document could be used to transfer authority back to the trustor.

What About Other Unknown Factors?

I customize my clients' estate plans to cover all known issues discovered during the time we discuss the family situation. I also add language to cover all the things that I see could go wrong in the future. All of the estate plans that I draft include a standby supplemental-needs trust. This is to protect beneficiaries if they later become disabled and have a need for government benefits.

I also include a provision for a Trust Protector. This allows the trust or will to adapt to unpredictable circumstances without requiring court involvement. Changes can be made with the help of an attorney. The Trust Protector can also correct errors in the trust or will. The way the Trust Protector works is by authorizing an independent trustee to appoint another independent person to make changes in the trust or will so that it may adapt to changes. The Trust Protector allows greater flexibility in accommodating changes in a beneficiary's circumstances or changes in the law.

When do you need your estate plan to work? The obvious answer is *when you die or become unable to handle your own affairs.* The problem, however, is that most estate plans are designed based on circumstances when the plan was created. Usually, those circumstances change.

In order to design a plan that will work when your family needs it, the preparer would ideally know the answers to the following questions:

When are you going to die or become incompetent?

- What will the laws be when you die?
- What assets will you own when you die?
- What will your family situation be when you die?
- Will all your assets be in the trust when you die?

Because the answers to these questions can (and probably will) change over time, it is important that your estate planning documents be drafted to be flexible so they can adapt to changes in circumstances and the law.

It is also important to review your estate plan every three years to make adjustments. I have been helping people protect those they love by designing their estate plans for over 25 years, but I have realized that there are things I can't predict or control.

That being said, my clients and I can make some educated guesses. And we can include many future possibilities in our plans. While no one can control everything, you can ensure your family's affairs will be handled in the manner you wish and that your family will be taken care of in the very best ways possible.

Key Takeaways:

1. Your "estate" is everything you own.

2. Wills and trusts are legal instruments that are crafted to let you decide exactly how you want your stuff divided and transferred to your chosen heirs.

3. A professional estate planning attorney can help you weigh the advantages of both instruments, then decide which best suits your needs—or if you need both.

4. Preplanning can save money and provide peace of mind for you and your loved ones.

Chapter Two

Handle-with-Care Stuff

When it comes to estate planning for a loved one with special needs, there is plenty to consider. No matter what happens to you, they'll likely need some kind of care for the rest of their lives. You know this perhaps better than anyone.

But how do you anticipate every unknown? Maybe your head is already spinning with questions like:

- How will they get the future resources they need?
- Will they be able to continue their government benefits?
- Who will make sure they are taken care of properly?
- What if something unforeseeable happens?
- How long will their inheritance last them?

Every expectant parent knows that early childhood years will be filled with new challenges, nights of interrupted sleep, days of laundry and doctor appointments. Next will come school, and a whole new round of concerns. Of course, it is all worth every bit of the effort and expense. No one could prepare those same excited parents for the shock of learning that their child has a condition that means he or she will have special needs for a lifetime.

Sleepless nights may last years instead of months. The doctors will be specialists and the schools will include meetings and individual education plans to determine how to achieve this child's best educational outcomes. These parents will become specialists themselves in areas they never imagined. They will spend a much higher percentage of their budget on the daily needs of their child than most other parents do. Other parents may anticipate their children becoming self-sufficient in time for the parents to focus their retirement years on themselves and grandchildren. These parents will plan their futures to include their child, always. This child will unquestionably be worth every bit of effort they expend. They will love him or her with great intensity, and they will be especially aware of the great need to plan for the time when they themselves will not be the ones providing the hands-on care that their special child will continue to need.

This chapter, we'll address these important questions and hopefully make it a little easier for you to protect your child's future. For questions about your specific situation, be sure to find an estate planning attorney who is experienced in special needs trusts. After reading this chapter, you should have confidence that a child with special needs and even the adult that the child will eventually become can be protected and cared for as well as possible.

Special Needs Planning

The first step in planning for the future is to look at the needs of the present, *then* you can anticipate future needs. For starters, it is important to review your life insurance and disability insurance to make sure that funds are available to take care of your child in case something happens to you. Then, be sure to document important information about your child.

One of our clients told me she started this process for her child with a three-ring notebook. She included everything a caregiver would need to know about her child, from infancy to the present day.

She had a tab labeled medical information, which included her child's diagnosis, illnesses, doctors' names, hospitals, clinics, pharmacies, and a list of medications. She also listed the medications that *did not work* as well as current ones.

Another tab was for developmental milestones, which included dates when her baby stopped nursing, when she ate solid foods, which foods she liked, which ones made her break out in a rash, etc. She recorded her child's age when she first rolled over. She recorded when she had expected her to sit up, but did not. She recorded when her daughter could finally sit alone—but had to wait several years before her child walked with crutches.

There was a tab for emergency contacts, which even included a description of her child's favorite stuffed animal, and the special cup without which she would not drink.

One section was devoted to financial information. This section provided information on life insurance and other assets that could be used to care for her daughter in the event that something happened to my client.

This notebook was perhaps one of the most important – not to mention, extremely loving -- elements in her planning process. After all, it was being used to organize all the information a caregiver would need to navigate doctor visits, clinic appointments, and agencies involved in her child's care.

It is important to plan ahead for any child, but it is even more urgent when the child has special needs. If one of your beneficiaries has a disability, it is vital to protect their inheritance with a special needs trust (also known as a supplemental needs trust).

Setting Up a Special Needs Trust

The special needs trust must be customized to the beneficiary's individual needs. This document specifies certain things the funds may be used for, and others that they may not.

It may specify, for example, "Trust funds may not be used to pay for any medical expenses covered by Medicare or Medicaid." This protects the funds in the trust from being considered when determining eligibility for Medicare or Medicaid. That leaves funds available for the many other needs not covered by those programs.

It is crucial to name a trustee who is familiar with government benefits. While helpful resources are provided, the application process can be daunting and the necessary reports and paperwork may be challenging. Someone who has navigated the system multiple times can make short work of something that may bring others to tears.

Another important item to have for the beneficiary is a comprehensive life plan. This will allow the trustee to maximize outside resources, including government benefits. It will also enable the trustee to ensure that the money lasts for the child's lifetime and provides for all non-medical needs.

Preparing a Letter of Intent

No one knows the day-to-day needs of your child better than you. Perhaps no one else ever will, but it is imperative that you communicate those daily needs to whomever will be caring for your child if and when you can't.

A letter of intent (or letter of instruction) is a valuable piece of any estate plan for families that have a child with a disability.

These letters give the trustee access to the child's doctors, medical needs, routines, interests, preferences, and abilities. The letters also help the trustee find resources in the community.

This knowledge will help improve your child's quality of life, make their transition easier, and help them enjoy a maximum degree of independence. This is also a smart way to help your trustee keep the child's routines intact. The letter needs to be updated every time the child's routine changes. The letter should contain the following information:

- *A typical day in the life of your child*: Include his or her favorite foods, music, books, television shows, online interests, and routines. Also include what brings them joy, what scares them, and what they hate. This is not a legal document. It is a way to guide future caregivers so as to ensure as little disruption as possible and avoid any upset in your child's life. If he or she has any special friends or favorite therapists, name them and say why your child responds well to that person, if you know. Mention anything special that works or does not work in managing behavioral issues.

- *Medical information*: Include current doctors, therapists, clinics, hospitals, medications, and therapies. Parents should explain how the medications are given and for what purpose. It is also helpful to list medications that *have not worked* in the past.

- *Educational activities your child has experienced*: Say what you envision about their potential. For instance, if your child can't read but has some artistic or musical talent, mention that.

- *Religious preferences and cultural traditions*: If your child attends church with the family, note the details, such as the time and locations of services or classes. If your family celebrates certain holidays, talk about those, including any food, music, or activities associated with each holiday.

- *Final arrangements*: Mention whether you have planned any funeral arrangements, cremation, burial, monument provisions, and/or religious services for your child. It is also helpful to have a list of relatives and friends with contact information and a note regarding any special relationships the child may have.

- *Parents' hopes and expressions of love for their child*: This is information that will be very valuable and inspirational to those who care for your child in the future, and will increase the likelihood of having your values expressed and lived out.

Parenting a child with special needs often calls for heroic effort. The suggestions in this chapter present emotional investment that may be difficult, but is absolutely worth the effort.

Mistakes Parents of Children with Special Needs Often Make

There are many misconceptions regarding special needs planning that can result in costly mistakes. Here are five things to avoid as you make careful plans for your child:

1. Counting on siblings to use their personal money to take care of the child with special needs

Parents may be tempted to rely on their other children to provide for a sibling with special needs. This can work temporarily, assuming the other children are financially secure and have money to spare. However, this isn't always the case. Siblings have their own expenses, unforeseen issues, and financial priorities.

2. Disinheriting the beneficiary with special needs

Many disabled people rely on SSI, Medicaid, or other government benefits. Parents may have been advised to disinherit their child with special needs to protect their public benefits. But these benefits rarely provide for more than basic needs. When a loved one requires (or is likely to require) governmental assistance to meet his or her basic needs, parents and/or grandparents should consider establishing a special needs trust.

3. Procrastinating

Because none of us know when we will die or become incapacitated, it is especially important that parents plan for a beneficiary with special needs early, just as they should for other dependents such as minor children. However, unlike most other beneficiaries, children with special needs may not be able to compensate for your failure to plan. Minor beneficiaries without special needs can obtain resources as they reach adulthood and can work to meet essential needs, but beneficiaries with special needs may never have that ability.

4. Ignoring the special needs when planning

Planning without the beneficiary's special needs in mind will probably render the beneficiary ineligible for essential government benefits. A properly designed special needs trust promotes happiness and comfort for the person with special needs, without sacrificing eligibility. Special needs may include: training and education, insurance, transportation, entertainment, vacations, and essential dietary needs.

5. Failing to properly fund and maintain the plan

When planning for a child with special needs, it is absolutely critical that there are sufficient assets available for the beneficiary throughout his or her lifetime. Life insurance can be used to provide this liquidity.

If you are a parent or caregiver with more questions about setting up a special needs trust for your loved one, get in touch with our team today.

Key Takeaways:

1. Planning for children with special needs should start with a thorough evaluation of present circumstances. Then consider what his or her future needs might include.

2. All the information you gather should be put into a document (or notebook) that is easily accessible to whomever will be in charge when you can't be. It should include medical information, developmental information, emergency contacts, financial information, and things only you know are important.

3. You may choose someone for direct care and another person to handle finances. Always designate alternates in case your first choices are not available when they are needed.

4. A special needs trust is vital to your planning, and the trustee should be someone with knowledge and experience of government programs and agencies.

5. No one knows your child like you do. That is why it is best to provide as much information as you can now—for those who will take care of your loved one in the event of your incapacity or death.

Chapter Three

Stuff Happens

Sometimes we worry about terrible things happening to us or to our families. After all, who can avoid the dire warnings that accompany the commercials for each of the medicines that have been prescribed for us, or may be in the future? We trust our doctor's judgment so we know we must take the medicine, but we can't help wondering which of the serious side effects may befall us.

There are also the frequent ads for "Memory Care" facilities built especially for the increasing numbers of people suffering Alzheimer's or other forms of dementia. As people age, it is an issue that becomes a realistic personal possibility. Everyone forgets things or has trouble recalling a name or word. Children are just learning, teens are distracted, and new moms claim to be having a "mommy moment," but seniors are sure to worry that each incident of forgetfulness is a forecast of Alzheimer's or another form of dementia.

The good news is, most of the things we worry about will never happen. Unfortunately, sometimes they do. The challenge then is to live without worrying excessively while also planning wisely for the problems that may come our way. Preparation can lessen the impact of difficult situations for our families and minimize our tendency to worry.

Alzheimer's and Dementia

Let's consider Alzheimer's and dementia and look at what you should do if you or your spouse is diagnosed with one of these conditions. There would be many changes in your life and many things requiring attention. Estate planning is one of them.

It is likely that your will, power of attorney, and health-care power of attorney name your spouse as the one who makes decisions if you are unable to make them (and vice versa). This arrangement makes sense if both spouses are healthy and capable.

If one or the other is diagnosed with Alzheimer's or any other kind of dementia, however, that person may not be capable of making clear decisions. Your documents would need to be changed to put someone else in charge, other than the spouse who has the diagnosis.

Sometimes people die out of order. We always assume that the healthy spouse will outlive the spouse with dementia, but it does not always work that way. If the healthy spouse dies first, and things are not updated, the spouse with dementia will be in charge of managing the money.

Creating a Supplemental Needs Trust

If you are like most people, your will probably leaves everything to your spouse upon your death. In the case of Alzheimer's or any kind of dementia, it would be better to create a supplemental needs trust for the diagnosed spouse.

That way, half of the assets can be protected for the diagnosed spouse in case he or she needs to go on Medicaid. It also provides a mechanism for someone other than the person suffering from Alzheimer's to be in control of the assets.

Creating an Asset Protection Trust

If you have not already preplanned for Medicaid benefits, it might be important to do so at this time. Sooner rather than later is definitely best. Assets that are transferred five years before someone needs Medicaid benefits are protected when determining eligibility.

Putting the assets in a trust also allows someone you choose to retain control over the assets. Plus, it ensures that the funds will be used as intended throughout the owner's lifetime.

Even if you and your spouse have no symptoms suggesting an immediate concern about dementia, having an asset protection trust can offer protection against other accidents or illnesses that may render one of you temporarily or permanently incapable of decision-making and financial management. Early planning also leaves fewer things to handle when facing incapacity.

Of course, no one wants to sit around thinking of all the bad things that *could* happen, but it is important to devote a small amount of time to deciding what you would want in worst-case scenarios. This will result in less stress should something actually happen. A good relationship with your estate planner will make it even easier should the need arise.

Key Takeaways:

1. Even in the most well-ordered of lives, accidents and illnesses occur.

2. We are constantly reminded of the dangers inherent in daily living, but worry does not make us safer.

3. Planning for worst-case scenarios will not prevent unfortunate things from happening, but it can lessen the impact on our families if they do occur.

4. Knowing that we are prepared with a special needs trust can alleviate our worries, freeing us to live our lives more fully.

Chapter Four

Stuff About What to Do If You Are Out of It

One of my clients was in a coma for three months after a serious car crash. He and his siblings owned a family business, and my client was the only signer on the business account. That was a problem.

In order to allow the business to function during his incapacity, his siblings had to get a guardianship over him. No one was able to sign checks for the business for over a month until the court appointed one of the brothers as his guardian. Fortunately, in this situation, no one contested the guardianship. (Contested guardianships can be extremely expensive and time-consuming.)

With a guardianship, the probate court appoints an attorney to represent the incapacitated person. Most of us, however, would rather make such a choice for ourselves. After all, we know whose expertise and values will best reflect our own. Planning ahead allows us to choose who will act on our behalf in the event that we can't act for ourselves. The attorney hired by the probate court to represent the incapacitated person is required to fight against the guardianship if the incapacitated person does not want the guardianship, even if he or she thinks that the guardianship would be in the incapacitated person's best interest. This can increase the expense and time to create the guardianship.

Even if there is no business operation at stake, there are other financial decisions that are just as important, and for which we are all responsible. Just think, who would legally be able to use your assets to pay your bills and manage your bank and credit card accounts?

These are everyday matters we take for granted, but your finances and credit rating could be put in serious jeopardy. Your family could suffer hardship and needless stress if you fail to prepare.

The Benefits of a Living Trust

A living trust is an excellent tool that allows you to make the wisest choices that will serve you well later on—if the need ever arises. For example, if my client who was recovering from a car crash had set up a living trust prior to becoming injured, and put his ownership of the trust into it, the trust would have named who he wanted to run the business (and sign the checks) during his incapacity.

By naming your successor trustees, you can also keep others who may not have your best interests at heart from trying to be appointed guardian. A spouse or a child may be a logical choice, or another trusted person who has the necessary ability. Here are five more benefits of a living trust:

More control

The living trust allows you to choose who manages your assets during your lifetime if you become incapacitated, and even after your death.

Interestingly, you may choose to name yourself as the trustee with the provision that a successor trustee takes over if you become unable to manage for yourself, in the case of incapacity or death. This is known as a revocable trust and it has the advantage of giving you the most freedom of choice during your lifetime.

Added privacy

Unlike a will, the living trust does not have to go through probate and there is no open record of its contents. No one knows what it says but you, and whomever you choose to disclose it to.

Easier management

A living trust can hold all of your assets, regardless of how you want them used or distributed. This can simplify management and allow for differences in how the assets are distributed to each beneficiary.

For example, perhaps one child is already of an age and ability to manage his or her share of the funds. Another is younger or has a disability that would necessitate having someone else manage his or her share of the inheritance. The living trust is extremely useful in arranging things to work the way you want, both during your lifetime and after your death.

Increased protection

The living trust can be crafted to protect assets from creditors, lawsuits, and divorce settlements. Plus, it is more difficult to challenge than a simple will.

It can also keep your beneficiaries from being disqualified for government benefits. Sometimes these are called supplemental needs trusts or special needs trusts. If you want trust funds to be outside of "countable assets" when applying for government benefits (such as Medicaid), you may need to choose an irrevocable trust. This simply means that the beneficiary could not be the trustee. Such a trust should be crafted by a professional who is experienced with government benefits.

Easier transitions

Although a living trust may initially cost more to create than a simple will, they usually cost less in the long run. The living trust will avoid court involvement if you become incompetent or pass away.

For example, a successor trustee can step in to keep a business running, pay the family's bills, or make decisions on your behalf in case of incapacity. It would not be necessary to go to court to obtain guardianship.

In the event of your death, the trustee could manage the trust and distribute funds according to your instructions. At a time when your family is grieving, it is an incredible gift to save them time, money, and the stressful process of probate.

Even if you have a will in place, call us at 940-387-8800 to reserve a place at one of our enjoyable seminars. All are packed with valuable information about living trusts. If you prefer, you can call to make an appointment. We will go over your existing plans and help you determine if a living trust might be right for you and your family.

What If You Don't Have a Trustee?

I have several clients who do not have children. In some cases, they have trouble deciding who will make financial decisions for them in the event they become incompetent.

For these clients who do not have any family members or friends whom they trust to make decisions for them, the trust department at a bank or investment firm could be a good choice for successor trustee. Before naming a trust department, however, the client should make sure that the chosen trust department does not have a minimum amount that must be in the trust before they are willing to be a trustee, and is willing to manage the type of assets that they own.

I had one client who appointed a larger bank as trustee. She was getting ready to have surgery and her husband was already incompetent. She called the bank's 1-800 number and left a message. It took three days for them to call her back. When she finally spoke to someone, she found out the bank would act as trustee only if there was over $3 million in assets.

They did not have that much money. If she had experienced complications during surgery and become incompetent or passed away, there would not have been a trustee in place to care for her husband.

In some cases, locally owned, smaller banks are willing to serve as trustee over trusts with under $3 million in assets. You may also ask your estate planner to suggest possible options for your particular situation.

I recommend that my clients interview the trust companies they are wanting to use. We had one bank tell the client that any rental property would be immediately sold. That client was wanting to keep the rental property and have it provide income for their childrens' lifetime. She found another bank who was willing to hire a property management company to oversee the rental property.

Planning Equals Protection

Some people find it difficult to talk about incapacity or death. Of course we all know we are going to die someday. We all hope it will be a quick and painless process. The thought of a serious incapacity can be downright daunting to think about. For your family's sake, however, you must prepare for these scenarios in your estate plan.

Here is how I explain it to my clients: When we buy insurance for our home, we don't imagine the house burning down or flooding or collapsing, and how terrible we would feel about losing everything. Even so, we know that such a calamity *could* happen. So, we do the responsible thing and buy insurance so our families will be cared for even if disaster strikes.

Likewise, when we plan for incapacity, we do so just in case it happens—so our families will be protected. Thinking about it does not make it more likely to happen. It does, however, lessen the impact on our families should we become incapacitated.

Problems with Powers of Attorney

A power of attorney (POA) can also be used to protect assets and handle business affairs in the event of incapacity. It simply names who can make financial decisions if we can't.

The courts (and many companies that accept powers of attorney) have determined that in order for someone to act under a POA, each action must be *specifically* listed. Fill-in-the-blank forms (or statutory forms) *are not* specific enough to allow people to do most things.

For example, the power to do Medicaid planning or veterans benefits planning or to care for your pets must be specifically listed in the power of attorney. It is almost impossible, however, to think of every important thing that might need handling during a period of incapacity. That makes the power of attorney a less adequate tool than a trust.

Another potential problem with a power of attorney is that it does not take away the incapacitated person's ability to revoke the power of attorney or to make financial decisions. Now that may seem like a good thing when we are of sound mind and hoping to stay that way. Still, we must remember that we are planning ahead *in case of incapacity*. We want to make sure that someone can make good choices for us when we can't. We also want to enable them to act when needed.

I know of several situations in which an incapacitated person was falling for scams. When the children tried to use the power of attorney, the incapacitated person tried to revoke the power of attorney. These cases ended up being contested guardianships, which cost the families thousands of dollars and much grief.

We must keep in mind the sobering fact that we will not necessarily know when we are no longer capable of making sound decisions.

For that reason, we should choose carefully someone we trust, be specific about how our incapacity should be determined, and responsibly make future plans. When the plans are in place, it is fine to hope that we will not need them!

Key Takeaways:

1. Accidents or illnesses can take away our ability to act responsibly and handle personal or business decisions. This can happen to anyone, at any age.

2. In the event of incapacity, someone will need to make decisions for you. You can choose the people who will act on your behalf by having the proper documents prepared.

3. Having a will or power of attorney will likely *not* be sufficient. Consult a qualified estate planner about preparing a living trust

that is designed to meet your particular needs in case of temporary or permanent incapacity.

Chapter Five

Stuff About Medical Decision-Making

We must consider the possibility that we could temporarily or permanently lose our ability to think or speak for ourselves. We hope that never happens, but we know that it can. We also must decide what to do about that possibility. The following is one such case:

Many years ago, a client came into my office and said, "My neighbor is in the hospital, unconscious. We have lived next door to each other for thirty years and we are best friends. I went to the hospital and the doctors won't tell me what is happening with her."

Apparently, the woman's son (whom she hadn't seen in over fifteen years) was making all her medical decisions.

The neighbor went on: "Is there a way for us to go to court and get me the right to make her medical decisions for her? I know that is what she would have wanted!"

Unfortunately, my answer had to be no. There was nothing we could do now, because her neighbor did not have the proper documents in place. If she had not wanted her son to make decisions for her, she could have signed documents indicating as much prior to becoming ill.

Without the proper documents in writing, immediate family members are the only ones allowed to make medical decisions.

Preventing Family Feuds

Because most of us are living longer than ever, more and more deaths are occurring in hospitals and nursing homes. This being the case, our odds of not being able to make decisions for ourselves—at some point in our lifetime—are very high. It would be wise for all of us to make our wishes known in case such a thing should happen.

The problems created by not having health care documents in place include the horrific struggle that was highlighted by Terry Schiavo's situation. You may remember that she was the woman in Florida who was on life support and her parents and her husband were arguing about whether she would have wanted to be kept alive in this manner.

She could have had documents in place to specify whether she wanted life support and under what circumstances. That family's grief was exacerbated by their opposing views. And their legal fees and years of feuding could have been avoided by a simple document prepared in advance.

A lot of people don't realize that they can even specify in that document that they do want life support. About 10% of my clients want to be kept alive under any circumstance. I actually had one client who wanted to have her brain frozen for future transplantation. Many choose to have life support in some circumstances, but not others.

There are no right or wrong answers here. Each person can decide for himself or herself before being incapacitated—and leave the proper documents where they are accessible.

The simple act of making the choice in advance and having proper documents prepared, keeps family members from being burdened with this great responsibility. It also protects our loved ones from having to deal with opposition during a very difficult time.

Directive to Physicians vs. DNRs

Understandably, many people get confused about the difference between a directive to physicians (or advance directive) and a do not resuscitate (DNR).

The example I use to explain the difference is this: Personally, I have a directive to physicians. If I have a heart attack, I want them to do CPR. If after doing CPR, the doctors say that they can put me on a ventilator but there is no hope of my recovering and having quality of life, I *don't* want to be put on life support.

If, however, the doctors say they can put me on a ventilator and I may recover and have a high probability of quality of life, I *do* want to be put on life support.

I want my family to ask the doctors, "What will that look like?" This will force the doctors to discuss the probabilities of quality of life, not just quantity. If I had a DNR, the paramedics would not even perform CPR. Each option should be carefully weighed, and one's choices clearly stated in the proper documents.

Unburdening Your Family

One problem with not having these documents in place is the guilt your family inevitably faces if life support is withdrawn. It is much easier on the family if they are aware of your wishes and can say, "Mom said she didn't want to be kept alive by machines in this type of situation."

I always encourage my clients to have the hard conversations with their family about under which circumstances they *would* and *would not* want life support.

This allows each individual the opportunity to let personal decisions be known, while also giving family members the chance to come to terms with choices that might be different from their own. The harder it is for one to have the conversation, the more important it probably is to have it.

An additional problem is not having a single decision-maker. If there are no documents in place, there may be more than one person under the law who has the right to make decisions for you.

If they don't agree, it can create conflict. Such conflicts can cause delays in making important decisions and can be very expensive if the decision-makers decide to argue in court. Often, if there is a conflict, the hospital and doctors take direction from whomever complains the loudest. That is why it is much better to make your own decisions and to put those decisions in writing.

Real-Life Scenarios

Recently, I had a situation involving a man with late-stage cancer. He was in the hospital and his family was deciding whether or not to continue life support. He told the doctor he did not want life support. His wife and most of his children agreed with him.

However, one of his sons told the doctor that Dad and Mom were incompetent. His only argument was that if they were competent, they would not be making the current decision to remove life support.

The patient's daughter called me to ask how to get the life support removed. Because I served for many years on a local hospital's ethics committee, I was aware of how ethics committees work. and I told her to ask for an ethics consultation.

The members of the ethics committee were able to get the family to agree to allow Dad to be placed in hospice care. If that had not worked, the next step would have been to file a lawsuit to get life support removed.

In another situation, a woman in her mid-eighties suffered congestive heart failure after surgery. Her family was shocked since the surgery had been considered "minor." After several days in the ICU, during which she was able to communicate, she went into a coma and her organs began shutting down.

Her husband and children all agreed to temporary life support when her doctors thought she might possibly recover. When informed that she would not likely recover, however, they agreed to remove life support.

One grandchild disagreed strongly. She tried to persuade other family members to object and soon everyone was upset. Finally, someone produced a document the patient had signed, specifically stating that she wanted to be on life support *only* if her doctors believed she could fully recover.

That convinced the grandchild, but she was comfortable with the decision only after the doctors assured the family that her grandmother would not suffer once life support was withdrawn. It turned out this was the real concern behind the grandchild's objection.

Although this particular situation was resolved, the family was thrown into emotional turmoil until the patient's advance directive was found.

Sometimes, even when people have prepared appropriate documents, they fail to have those papers with them when they are needed. On admission to the hospital, staff will ask if the patient has a directive to physicians. They will then check a box saying you have one. But if they don't have a copy, no one will know your wishes regarding life support.

That is why we recommend asking your estate planning attorney for a health emergency card. It provides doctors and hospital staff access to important health care documents so they know who has been appointed to oversee your decisions if you can't, and how to get in touch with them.

Key Takeaways:

1. Do your own soul-searching. Decide what you want your physicians to do in case of emergencies.

2. Discuss your decisions with your family and close friends.

3. Prepare the appropriate documents as soon as possible.

4. Make sure your physicians and health care providers—as well as your appointed decision-makers—have access to the necessary documents.

Chapter Six

HIPAA and Privacy Stuff

Health Insurance Portability and Accountability Act (HIPAA) is the privacy law that protects our medical records. That is a good thing, but it can keep loved ones from being able to check on you in the hospital. It is important to understand how the law works and how you can participate in making it work for you.

We have become used to protecting information regarding our credit cards and bank accounts. But many of us are not aware that we need to take equal precautions to protect our medical information from theft or fraud.

Imagine needing a knee replacement and having your insurance company deny the benefit. Later, you find out your medical records show that both knees have already been replaced— for someone pretending to be you!

HIPAA goes a long way toward preventing such fraud. It is intended to protect personal information from identity theft or public disclosure.

Unfortunately, it may also dramatically impair your estate plan in several unforeseen and unintended ways.

You may have noticed that your doctor, pharmacy, and other health care providers now ask you to sign a receipt for their "Notice of Privacy Practices." You may have even thought of it as yet another meaningless form that you sign after only briefly scanning those endless "terms and conditions." These documents are more important than you might think.

Planning with HIPAA in Mind

HIPAA was passed by Congress to provide a secure way for health information to be safely passed between health care providers, insurance companies, and specified individuals.

In the event that any health information is wrongfully disclosed by your health care provider, HIPAA imposes fines of up to $250,000, as well as jail time of up to 10 years. You can see why this would motivate your medical providers to be very careful about how they share your medical information!

Health care providers can't give information about you or your health to anyone, regardless of the reason, without your express permission.

HIPAA allows you to give permission to your doctors and other health care providers to share parts or all of your medical information with specific others, such as a spouse, relative, or caregiver.

Unfortunately, HIPAA has not provided one standard form for such authorization. Doctors and hospitals hire attorneys to make sure their privacy authorizations comply with HIPAA. Their attorneys tell each of them, "If you have your patients sign the form that I designed, then you can protect yourself from being sued."

Doctors and hospitals are going to be nervous about accepting any other form. This may prove inconvenient for us but is quite understandable if we look at it from their point of view.

An Important Provision

As complicated as all of this may seem, there are things you can do to protect your privacy *and* allow those you trust to get information when needed.

I include a provision in any living trust, will, general power of attorney and medical power of attorney that permits your successor trustee or agent to sign a valid authorization on your behalf. That way, they can sign whatever form the doctor or hospital uses if you are unable to do so yourself.

This provision is important because it allows your family members to receive the necessary information when your emergency happens. The trusts that I draft also provide that once someone accepts the role of trustee, he or she needs to sign an authorization for the next in line to review his or her medical records. That way, if the successor trustee becomes incompetent, it is easy for the next trustee to step in.

Imagine that your mother or father experiences an accident or sudden illness. If the other parent is also incapacitated, the medical staff may not be able to give family members information. That little piece of paper authorizing someone to sign the HIPAA release on behalf of the patient would be an instant, easy solution. Without it, even children may not be able to get the information they desperately need at a difficult time.

This is especially important if you are caring for a relative who is disabled. Suppose you are caring for a sibling who needs assistance getting to the doctor and a variety of supportive medical therapies. Your sibling may be able to sign the HIPAA form now, but what if they have a medical event or injury that prevents them from signing later?

Having the appropriate forms in place before an emergency will not only give you peace of mind, but will free you to use your energy and resources on their behalf when they need it most.

Key Takeaways:

1. HIPAA law protects you from medical fraud, invasion of privacy, and misuse of your medical records and information.

2. HIPAA forms provided by your health care providers allow you to share all or part of your health records and information with specific individuals, providers, and agencies designated by you.

3. A special provision in your living trust may be your best solution. You may use this provision to name a person (and even an

alternate) who can sign such a form for you when you can't. This protects you in case you need an updated form, or if you have to use a new physician or hospital in an emergency. Remember, HIPAA does not provide uniform documents.

4. Have an attorney prepare a HIPAA form and add provisions to your financial and medical power of attorney that allow your chosen agent to sign whatever forms the doctor or hospital needs signed.

Chapter Seven

Long-Term Care Stuff

The younger we are, the more likely we are to act as if we are going to live forever. At some point, we accept that death is inevitable. Even then, we probably see it as a far-off truth rather than an immediate concern. What is even more difficult for us to imagine is the possibility that we may become unable to care for ourselves on a daily basis. Not so long ago, families were the only resource for those needing long-term care. Only a few generations ago came the common use of Assisted Living and Skilled Nursing Care facilities. Now we are jokingly warned to be kind to our children, because they will probably choose our nursing homes!

The longer we live, the greater the chances that we will need some type of long-term care. That care may come from a combination of family members, professional caregivers, adult day care centers, assisted living facilities, nursing homes, or even hospice.

No one wants to need long-term care, but it is a good idea to have a plan in place, just in case such help is ever needed.

Long-term planning will include the usual safety nets: health insurance, long-term care insurance, and savings accounts. With the rising cost of medical care, home health care, assisted living and skilled nursing care, health insurance and personal savings accounts may not be nearly enough. Fortunately, several programs are available to help. The two most commonly used resources are veterans benefits and Medicaid.

Qualifying for Veterans Benefits

As of 2020, a married veteran can qualify for $2,266 per month in a pension if they need aid and attendance. A single veteran can qualify for roughly $1,912 per month, and the widow of a veteran can qualify for $1,230 per month. Here are some of the qualifying factors to receive VA benefits:

The veteran must have served at least 90 days, and at least one of those days needs to have been during a defined period of war.

- The veteran must have a medical need and must require help with activities of daily living (bathing, dressing, toileting, etc.).
- Current net worth maximum (as of 2020) is $128,640.00. Net worth is defined as a sum of assets and annual income minus medical expenses, which can include the cost of home health care, assisted living, and nursing home care.

Additionally, the exemption for a homestead is limited to two acres, unless the remainder of the property is deemed unmarketable. Veterans might want to consider making gifts to protect more than two acres or assets over the net worth maximum to protect the family farm.

The veteran can also make a gift to a family member or friend with the expectation that the money will be used to take care of the veteran's needs later in life. That is a reasonable solution, but I always recommend the gift be placed in a trust. This assures that everyone is clear that the money is protected for the veteran's benefit. (Beginning October 18, 2018, there is a three-year "look back" for any gifts made after that date.)

The trust money is further protected from divorce, creditors, and lawsuits. The trust also provides a clear plan as to who will manage the money in case something happens to the first trustee.

Gifting Wisely

When I first started practicing law decades ago, a client taught me the importance of setting up a trust to protect gifted assets. When I first met my client, she was 80 years old and receiving food stamps and Section 8 housing. Back when she had turned 65, she gifted a million dollars to her son so the government would not take the money if she ever had to go into a nursing home.

Her son was a wonderful guy and she had no doubt he would take care of her and use the money for her care. Unfortunately, she failed to consider her daughter-in-law.

Sadly, her son was killed in a car crash, whereupon the daughter-in-law basically said, "Thank you for the money. I can use it to raise your son's children."

My client even took her daughter-in-law to court to try to recover the million dollars, but the court said, "Because you gave it to your son with no strings attached, there is no way for you to get it back."

Even if you have the best children in the world, you *must* consider what would happen if they pass away or become disabled. Eventually, the money will go to someone who may not do the right thing. If money is gifted outside of a trust, there is no assurance that the money will be used as the giver intends. It is far better to specify its use in a trust than to leave it to chance.

Sharing the Caregiving Load

I once had a case involving a veteran's wife whose husband had Alzheimer's. She was becoming exhausted from caring for him. As she wasn't ready to put him into a nursing home, I helped her to get approximately $1,900 per month to use toward his home health care.

Sometimes, VA benefits can be a lifesaver for the spouse who is taking care of the veteran. I have known two caregiver spouses who died before the spouse that they were taking care of because of exhaustion. Additional help can literally be a lifesaver. I always encourage spouses to consider these resources.

One of the things I love about working with veterans benefits is how big a difference they can make for a family. The veteran who needs aid and attendance can afford to spend more on care, without increasing his or her out-of-pocket expenditures. Plus, the caregiver(s) can afford some much-needed help.

Medicaid Benefits

Medicaid is another way to get the federal government to help pay for skilled nursing care. There are, of course, asset and income requirements. With a married couple, there are ways to protect all of the assets, and with a single person we can usually protect about half of the assets.

The first lady I helped with Medicaid was 65 years old. Her husband needed to go into a nursing home, but she was healthy enough to stay in independent living. They had about $300,000 they had saved during the course of their marriage.

Under the Medicaid rules—and without advance planning—she was allowed to keep around $100,000 and the rest would have to be spent before he could qualify for Medicaid. Her rent in independent living was approximately $36,000 per year.

She asked a very important question: "What happens when I am 68, and have spent all my money on rent?" Through advance planning, we were able to protect the full $300,000.

You *must* have these conversations with your estate planning attorney early and often. If you don't, you could be left without the quality care you or your spouse desperately need.

Long-Term Care Insurance

Another option for paying for long-term care is long-term care insurance, which can help protect assets against the high cost of extended care. It can also help you stretch your income to pay for living expenses until you qualify for Medicaid.

Personally, I have life insurance with a long-term care rider. This allows me to protect my assets in case long-term care is needed. If it is not needed, the policy will provide money to my family upon my death.

Medicaid Preplanning

If you want to protect your assets from future long-term care costs and do not qualify for long-term care insurance, another option is Medicaid preplanning. Using this strategy, you are able to give your assets to a Medicaid Asset Protection Trust controlled by someone you trust. If the transfer of assets occurs at least five years before application for Medicaid, the funds will not be considered, and they may be used to pay for other needs while Medicaid covers basic medical needs, including nursing home care, if necessary.

It is important to gather as many facts as possible ahead of time, and to prepare any necessary documents you might need. Then be sure to share and discuss these plans with everyone involved.

Dealing with programs such as veterans benefits and Medicaid can be complicated, but with a little help, it need not be overwhelming. Planning ahead—and with an experienced professional—reduces stress and ensures the best possible results.

Key Takeaways:

1. Many of us will need long-term care, which may seriously impact our financial resources.

2. Veterans benefits are available to those who have served in the military at least 90 days, one of which was in a defined period of war.

3. Medicaid benefits are federally subsidized and administered by the state. There are income and asset requirements, but you should not assume that you would not qualify.

4. A Medicaid Asset Protection Trust should be considered when planning for long-term care.

5. Early planning can make all the difference in making sure that you have the resources you need, when you need them.

Chapter Eight

Stuff to Protect Your Children

Most of us realize that we can't control everything. We do the best we can to make wise decisions, but some things are not within our total control. This is even truer when it comes to our children. We do have some control, and we can definitely affect the direction and outcomes of many things pertaining to them, but not everything.

Among the most important tasks for those of us who have children under the age of eighteen is determining who will raise our children in the event of our death or disability.

When I first started practicing law, I did not have children and I did not understand how difficult it was for a parent to make this kind of decision. Now that I have boys of my own, I understand how hard it is to think of anyone else raising one's children.

But as every parent knows, we can't avoid tough decisions just because they make us uncomfortable. Another important decision we must make is about how we will provide money for our children's needs—and who will manage those funds.

Sometimes the same person will be entrusted with both responsibilities. But oftentimes, the talents required for each of these jobs are found in different people. You may have a family member who is great with kids and who has a loving relationship with your children. That person may not manage finances as easily.

It may be helpful, in that case, to appoint a different person or a corporate trustee to handle the money. You have the option to set it up according to what you think is the best choice for your family.

Providing for Minor Children

Anyone who has raised a child to adulthood can, and will, be sure to tell the young parents how many more decisions await and how many more important ways you will be required to protect your child.

Even though it is a tough topic, you must ask yourself the following questions and create a plan for your child's future:

- Who will raise your children and make decisions for them if you can't?

- Who will instill in them the values you want passed on to them?

- Who will provide for them financially, or manage a trust if one is set up for them?

- In many families, one (or both) of the spouses has been married previously. This may affect decisions about guardianship, and extra care may be needed to maintain relationships between siblings and stepparents. Who will handle this, and how?

- If you are a single parent, a surviving biological parent would likely be named guardian unless they were proven unfit. That person would also likely be given control over the minor child's inheritance until they reach eighteen. This can be changed if you do not want the biological parent in charge of the money. Do you have the proper documents in place in this scenario?

Rather than leaving matters to chance, it is better to plan. It helps to remember that the person who provides the hands-on care need not be the same person who manages the money for a minor child.

It is wise to make contingency plans that cover the possibility of losing one or the other parent, as well as the possibility of losing both. These are not fun considerations, but they are as at least as important as choosing a good car seat or a good school for your child.

No one can make decisions for your child's future better than you. Talk to your estate planning attorney about any particular questions you have or provisions you'd like to include regarding the care of your children.

Transferring Assets to Your Children

In addition to plans for rearing your children, there is the separate matter of passing on money and other assets to them. Many people think in terms of dividing assets equally among children, with grandchildren receiving portions that would have gone to any children who preceded their parents in death.

It is becoming more common, however, for some to choose more customized approaches to take care of the particular needs or circumstances of their families.

For example, parents may set up and fund a supplemental needs trust for a child who is disabled and will need to rely on government programs for long-term medical needs and assistance with daily living. Such a trust would protect the child's inheritance from being considered in an eligibility determination for benefits. The trust would then support the child's other needs and ensure a better quality of life.

Parents may also leave some assets based on the individual preferences of the recipients. One child may want the family farm, while another would prefer getting stock certificates. One adult child, when asked by her parents what she would want, answered that she wanted only the family photographs and access to her father's genealogical research on their family tree.

It took some convincing that she meant it, but indeed that is what was important to her. She promised to make digital copies of all the pictures available to the rest of the family. The oldest son wanted his father's extensive tool collection.

In that family, two of the children suggested that the parents leave the family home to the only child who lived in close proximity, but did not yet own a home. The nearby child was also in a position to give the parents "hands-on" assistance whenever needed.

The only way parents can possibly know what their children want is to have honest discussions with them about these matters.

Why This Matters So Much

Whether our children are minors or adults, whether they are responsible or not, whether they are healthy and independent or disabled, they mean the world to us. Whether we, as parents, have a lot of assets or very few, we will protect our children best by planning for the possibility of our absence or disability.

One family I knew had a simple will. Upon the death of one of the parents, the other would inherit everything. When the second parent died, the entire estate would be divided equally between their four children.

It sounded fair and reasonable. One child, however, had a history of alcohol and drug abuse. His portion of the inheritance gave him money to indulge in the habits his parents had tried so hard to help him overcome. Even though he had been clean and sober for 20 years, he decided to use part of his inheritance to purchase really expensive drugs that he couldn't afford back when he was using. He passed away from an overdose.

Another child had a condition that impaired his mental and physical abilities. He needed lifelong care as well as someone to manage his finances. His inheritance made him ineligible for the government-sponsored benefits he had been receiving. They were stopped until most of his inheritance had been "spent down." He had to wait several months before he was able to resume his physical and occupational therapy because there was a waiting list for those services.

The other two siblings received their money. One bought a luxury automobile and some other indulgences. The other daughter was more conservative in her spending, but lost most of it in a divorce.

Within ten years, none of the children had any of the money left, or anything of value they had purchased with it. This story could have been much different if the family had known about some better choices in estate planning.

Again, trusts can be used to protect our heirs from unwise spending, divorce, lawsuits, and bankruptcy. They can even be crafted so that supplemental needs trusts provide for those requiring long-term or lifelong care.

Grandchildren and Heritage Trusts

When grandchildren are involved, a Heritage Trust may be a good choice. This trust ensures that the money passes to the grandchildren, rather than your child's spouse.

If the money were left to a son or daughter without a trust, for example, the child would likely leave it to their spouse. The "in-law" could then remarry.

Would it not only be possible, but likely, that the money would end up in the hands of a stepparent rather than being left to the grandchildren of the original donors? A Heritage Trust would take care of any scenario without awkward choices or unnecessarily hurt feelings.

I can design a Heritage Trust for my clients that protects even the least capable and irresponsible heir, as well as the wisest and most mature heir. It can protect them from creditors, lawsuits, and divorce. If the child is mature enough and responsible, he or she can even be named as their own trustee and have access to the money, yet still be protected from creditors, lawsuits, and divorce.

Specifying Guardianship

I know of two sets of grandparents who are not speaking to each other because their son and daughter-in-law did not specify a guardian. The parents died suddenly, and the grandparents ended up in a custody battle over the grandchildren.

The court awarded custody of the grandchildren to one set of grandparents, and the grandparents who lost the custody battle do not get to see their grandchildren. So, the children not only lost their parents, but they also needlessly lost a set of grandparents (and probably numerous other relatives on that side of the family as well).

This could have been avoided if the parents had named a guardian. Sure, someone may have felt slighted that another had been chosen, but that would have been a minor upset compared to the ravages of a custody battle.

As parents, we must take a sober look at what we *can* and *should* do when it comes to passing assets on to our children. It is not just a matter of giving or not giving. It is a matter of choosing the best way to provide for our kids (and grandkids) when we are no longer around.

Key Takeaways:

1. Your documents should be customized to your individual family situation.

2. We can't control every aspect of our children's lives, but we can make wise choices (and put them in writing) that will greatly affect their lives.

3. We can and should name the people we wish to raise our children in the event of our death or disability.

4. It is equally important to provide funds for the rearing of our children and to name who should manage those funds.

5. There are different types of wills and trusts that make it possible to provide specific instructions that meet the needs of each particular family member. A competent estate planning attorney is an invaluable partner in helping you find your best options.

Chapter Nine

Important Stuff

Traditional estate plans focus almost exclusively on transferring assets, reducing taxes, and minimizing administrative costs. More comprehensive estate plans add ethical wills, incentive trusts, and involve your children in the process.

What Is an Ethical Will?

An ethical will is a nonlegal document that allows a person to share his or her personal values, life lessons, family history, family traditions, expectations for the future, dreams and hopes, as well as religious and spiritual ideas. It may include anything else considered important for that person to convey to family and friends.

Ethical wills can also provide future generations with an individual's health history, in order to inform descendants of potential health risks they could possibly be facing later in life.

Ethical Wills are a tradition that can even be found in the Old and New Testaments of the Bible. You may think you have passed this information on throughout your lifetime, but it will have the additional advantage of being available to future generations as well. Personal stories are particularly effective tools for passing on valuable information and helpful guidance to others.

This document may be written at various stages in life and may be amended at any time throughout an individual's lifetime.

Ethical wills have been written by couples who are engaged to be married, women and men who are welcoming newborns into their lives, families that are growing in size, middle-aged singles, and married couples, as well as individuals facing terminal or life-threatening illnesses. If you have not created an ethical will, the best time to start working on one is now.

Why Make an Ethical Will?

Ethical wills allow an individual to be remembered for what he or she values in life. It enables the person to tell the story of their unique experience to loved ones, and have it last forever. Anyone who has been the lucky recipient of such a thoughtful gift can tell you how special and inspiring it is to have such a treasure.

This document is also an excellent place to recognize those who have contributed to your life. You may also wish to express your appreciation for various members of your family or special friends, letting them know how much they mean to you.

An ethical will can even help an individual come to terms with his or her mortality. It facilitates closure by providing family and friends with the ideals and passions by which one has lived, and the reasons why.

It can also help you to condense personal experiences into life lessons, which can be passed down for generations to come. After all is said and done, it could become one of the most appreciated contributions you make to your family and friends.

Incentive Trusts

It is important to make sure your will or trust expresses your values. You can add incentives for behaviors you want to encourage, such as staying off drugs, being employed, or completing a college education.

I have drafted incentive trusts that reward being gainfully employed by matching the beneficiary's salary. Trusts can also be drafted to include drug or alcohol testing, and bonuses for graduating from college or achieving certain grades. You can reward any behavior you want to encourage.

Family Meetings

At a client's request, I can meet with their children to discuss what the parents have set up and explain why it is set up that way. This is an opportunity to meet the children in a stress-free environment. Such a meeting has the added benefit of letting them know whom to call when death or disability occurs.

I also talk to families about the fact that one of the stages of grief is anger, and that we sometimes take that anger out on those closest to us. I tell them how very important it is to their parents that there won't be any conflict after they are gone.

Lessons from My Grandparents

Not long ago, I was speaking at a seminar about a lesson I learned from my grandparents: Whenever they sent us a check, my grandmother always insisted that we use the money for something practical and that we write a thank-you note. When my grandfather passed away and left me some money, my first thought was wondering what practical thing I was going to spend the money on.

One of the people at the seminar asked me, "Who are you going to write the thank-you note to?" That got me thinking. I am writing this portion of the book as my thank-you note. I am so very grateful that my grandparents taught me to be responsible with money.

Another person asked me, "What was the most meaningful gift they ever gave you?" That prompted me to remember several special gifts along the years. My grandparents sold toys wholesale to stores like Eckerd's. Eckerd's were like Walgreens or CVS and they had a toy aisle. My grandparents had a toy warehouse with samples of all the different toys. It was fun as a kid to be able to see all the toys and play with them before purchasing them.

I learned the difference between how cool the toys looked on television and how they actually felt to play with in person. For my birthday for several years, they let me pick any toy I wanted from the warehouse. I always wanted the gumball machine just because I wanted the gum out of it.

My grandparents and parents explained to me that this was not a practical choice because the other toys would be more fun, while gum was available outside the machine. This was a child-sized lesson that has lasted me a lifetime.

Key Takeaways:

1. A meeting with parents and their children has several benefits:

   - It ensures the children know what their parents have set up in their estate plan.

   - It gives the children an opportunity to ask any questions they may have and provides a professional atmosphere in which to handle any issues that may arise.

   - It allows the children to get acquainted and comfortable with the person they will rely on to provide documents and assistance at a time of disability or death in the family.

2. Incentive trusts provide an effective way to encourage the behaviors you value. They ensure your money does not enable undesirable habits or choices that may be tempting to the

recipients. The incentive trust encourages positive behaviors and desired outcomes.

3   Ethical wills are:

- Intended to pass on important information such as health histories, religious beliefs, moral values, life experiences, lessons learned, hopes, dreams, gratitude, and appreciation for loved ones. They are nonlegal documents and may be as formal or informal as the client desires.

- Easily updated as families grow and when new issues, concerns, and experiences make changes necessary.

- Designed to be a valuable influence on others, providing moral and spiritual guidance.

- Excellent tools for leaving a treasure trove of personal and family information to future generations.

Chapter Ten

Retirement Stuff

Retirement funds are designed to encourage people to save money while they are still working. The money saved in such a fund is sometimes matched by employers, and usually protected from taxes until the money is withdrawn.

The funds are invested and earn interest or dividends. Eventually the funds provide for the owner and are taxed at the owner's current tax rate. This plan works really well in providing financial stability for retirement.

The retirement account, however, is not the only means of financial support during retirement. Retiring couples often have additional assets such as stocks, bonds, individual savings accounts, investment properties, and of course their homes and Social Security Income.

Those wise in financial management will usually tap into their other available resources while letting the retirement account accrue maximum earnings to avoid unnecessary taxation. Eventually, there are requirements for minimum withdrawals, but the major portion of the account can continue to grow and earn rather than be diminished by taxes.

Retirement Account Beneficiaries

If you can save your retirement account funds to be spent last, they are likely to be the largest asset in your estate. Even if those funds go to a surviving spouse, they will continue to be protected from taxation, creditors, and lawsuits—just as they were in original ownership.

When a beneficiary who is not the spouse inherits a retirement account, that beneficiary can withdraw funds over 10 years or his or her lifetime, being taxed only on the amount withdrawn. See Appendix XV for details on how the retirement accounts will be withdrawn under the SECURE Act.

Unfortunately, most beneficiaries do not realize the tax benefit of consulting with an attorney, accountant and financial advisor on the timing of withdrawals to minimize income taxes. They make the mistake of withdrawing the entire amount immediately. The result can be costly because it is usually taxed at a higher rate. This is especially true if the beneficiary is still working full time.

Even more serious than losing this tax advantage is losing the protections against creditors, lawsuits, and bankruptcy. The funds would also become vulnerable to being considered in the division of assets in a divorce.

Retirement Plan Trusts

Congress did not contemplate asset protection for anyone other than the worker or his or her spouse. It is therefore wise for the owner to anticipate this need by means of a trust.

Another major problem in planning for qualified plans and IRAs is that beneficiaries may quickly spend the money in the retirement accounts. Retirement plans are designed to provide maximum benefit to those who withdraw funds at a modest rate over time. The individual who initially created the retirement plan often does not take out more than the required minimum distributions. They use the funds to supplement other income. Their beneficiaries, however, might not feel so restrained. They may view retirement plans in the same way they would view a lottery win.

Sometimes the large amount of money, suddenly available, is tempting. If the money is spent, the remaining funds gain less through interest, and the amount spent carries a higher tax burden. This decreases the total value of the legacy.

The better way to handle retirement accounts is to place them in a retirement plan trust. These trusts protect the retirement accounts from a beneficiary's divorce, creditors, and lawsuits. Plus, they encourage the beneficiary to withdraw the funds slowly, over his or her lifetime. We can still have these benefits even after the passage of the SECURE Act, See Appendix XV for details.

Key Takeaways:

Establishing a Retirement Plan Trust and naming it as the beneficiary of an IRA or qualified plan can provide a number of benefits:

1. Spendthrift protection: Protects the individual trust beneficiary from his or her temptation to unwisely manage the retirement money.

2. Predator protection: Even if the individual beneficiary does not have spendthrift tendencies, there are many out there whose interests lie in separating the beneficiary from their money and property.

3. Creditor protection: Ours is a litigious society in which we never know who is going to be the target of a lawsuit. A trust makes the beneficiary a less attractive "target."

4. Divorce protection: With the national divorce rate above 50 percent, it is impossible to determine which marriages will stand the test of time. A Retirement Plan Trust keeps the inherited IRA from being divided or even lost in a divorce.

5. Government benefits protection: As with divorce, whether a healthy beneficiary will suffer some catastrophe that makes him or her dependent on needs-based government programs is unpredictable. Inheriting an IRA can easily disqualify someone from receiving needs-based government benefits until the IRA is

exhausted. On the other hand, even with the help of government benefits, a protected trust can provide for additional needs.

6. Consistent investment management: Allows the current investment advisors to continue to be involved.

7. Estate planning: Control over use of the retirement plan/IRA assets (e.g., to   fund education, start a business, buy the beneficiary's first home, or in the case of a blended family, to prevent diversion away from the owner/participant's descendants).

Chapter Eleven

Finding Stuff and Organizing Stuff

How many times have you needed an important document and lost track of where you put it? How many times have you said, "I have got to get more organized!"? If you smiled or groaned over these questions, you are not alone!

One of the biggest factors causing delays and increased cost during estate settlement is the inability to locate assets. That is why we encourage our clients to have a list of their assets showing where they are located, especially if they hide money.

If no such list is available, Goodwill or whoever buys your house will end up with the money. I actually heard someone on the radio telling people to buy silver bars and bury them in the backyard. That is not advice I would offer, but it does happen.

One of our clients was cleaning out her mother's freezer and getting ready to throw out what she thought was meat wrapped in aluminum foil. Noticing it did not weigh as much as it should, she opened up the foil and found thousands of dollars in "cold cash."

In another example, a trust company was getting a house ready for sale when a neighborhood dog dug up a coffee can in the backyard. In that coffee can they found a thousand dollars. Then more coffee cans surfaced. They found over a hundred thousand dollars in the backyard!

Discovering Unclaimed Funds

Many people have paid-up life insurance policies that their families know nothing about. In fact, five percent of life insurance policies that mature (meaning someone has died) go unclaimed. Sometimes families find out there is life insurance only after they receive a premium notice. Other times, they may never know.

If you have a paid-up life insurance policy, be sure to tell your family. Better still, leave a detailed record of it in your list of assets and make sure your family knows where to find the list.

I advise my clients who have lost a loved one to check the unclaimed funds in every state where their loved one has lived or might have opened a bank account. I recommend they check when the loved one passes away and again seven years later.

It is much kinder to include this information on your all-important asset list. This makes things a lot easier on your family when they know where to find your assets. Yes, it takes effort to make a list of all the assets and where to locate information about each one. It is an important thing to do, though, and will save your family a great deal of effort in the long run. The list also gives them the assurance that they haven't missed anything.

Decide where this list will be so that it is secure, but available to the person or persons who will be dealing with your affairs in the event of your incapacity or death.

What to Include in Your Asset List

Use the list below to help you gather all the information you need. You do not have to find everything today, just make sure it is a priority. Then tell your family and your attorney where to find your list.

Remember—computers crash. So, print out and safely store updated copies whenever you make a change. Here is what to include:

- *Insurance policies*: Name of insurance company, address and phone number, name of insured, name of beneficiary, amount of benefit, date of purchase, whether it is paid up—or the amount and frequency of premiums and method of payment.

- *Bank accounts*: Name and address of bank, account type, name and number (list each account). If you use online banking, be sure to note that information, but do not leave user ID and password information where someone might find them accidentally. (Don't tape it to the side of your computer!) Put it on the list and secure the list.

- *Deposit boxes*: Bank name and address, contents of the box, access information.

- *Retirement accounts*: Name of financial institution, name of account holder and account number.

- *Houses*: Deed and mortgage information, purchase date and price, improvements after purchase, warranties, tax information, and dates paid. Also be sure to list vacation homes or timeshare properties.

- *Household contents*: Furniture and appliances, valuable paintings, jewelry, china, crystal, silver, etc. Include dates purchased and value at time of purchase (or current known value).

- *Cars*: Make, model, and VIN number of each vehicle, lien holder (if any), payments (if applicable), and repair history.

- *Anything else you own*: Boats, recreational vehicles, motorcycles, equipment, tools, and business interests.

- *Receivables*: If you have loaned money or property, list the details of the loan and your wishes regarding repayment. Do you expect your estate to receive the repayment or do you wish to forgive the debt?

- *Passwords*: List of all passwords and login information for all online accounts.

- *Where you hide money*: List the location and amount.

Key Takeaways:

1. Treasure hunting is a fun game for children, but locating your assets and important documents will be serious business when someone else is responsible for taking care of them.

2. Use the suggestions in this chapter to create an asset list with important information to help those who will handle your affairs if you can't. If you feel the job is too overwhelming, ask for help from the person you have chosen to handle your affairs, or your estate planning attorney.

3. Your family will surely appreciate your efforts. It is a very loving thing to do!

Chapter Twelve

Second Marriage Stuff

After a divorce or the death of a spouse, it is common for individuals to marry again. This often creates a circumstance of each spouse having children from a previous marriage blending with children from the current marriage. There can also be adopted children being reared with birth children. Blending a family is not always easy, though, as each situation brings its own blessings and challenges.

One of the challenges that must be considered is how the estate plan will be crafted to meet the current couple's obligations and wishes for the family members involved. Neglecting this issue should not even be considered an option. In the event of an unexpected illness, incapacity, or death, such neglect could lead to family fights.

Lack of planning and preparation has caused some well-publicized family feuds that make headlines. Local courts often deal with families torn apart by issues that could and should have been avoided. The best way to have a smooth transition upon disability or death is to create a comprehensive strategy *before* you are no longer able to execute the papers.

Love and Remarriage

A second marriage may result in cordial, but sometimes not-so-close step-relations. Even if a couple is happily married, their children are not always as happy. They may merely tolerate each other until the biological parent dies or becomes disabled.

Complications and difficulties are especially likely when the spouse who has the majority of assets dies first. If a parent is not careful, his or her children may unintentionally be disinherited. If the children are protected, the surviving spouse may be disinherited.

Either scenario may be the intended choice, or a person could choose an option that includes both spouse and children.

A special plan for a blended family would include a prenuptial agreement and a postnuptial agreement, along with a fully funded, revocable living trust. This would ensure that the assets would be distributed as intended and all parties would know the wishes of the benefactor.

Children from Previous Marriages

If you have children from a previous marriage and don't have a will, when you die your property will be co-owned by your current spouse and your biological children. In some cases that could be fine, but often it is not.

I had a client several years ago whose husband owned a parcel of land prior to the marriage. After they married, the couple constructed a building on the property and the wife worked full-time creating a business on the land. Her husband died suddenly, without a will. When the probate court judge asked her if her husband had a will, the wife responded, "No, he wasn't planning on dying."

None of us are planning on dying and proper planning does not increase your odds of passing away. Under the laws of intestate succession, she was entitled to a third of the income from the business and a third of the proceeds when the property was sold. This is probably not what her husband intended, and certainly not what she wanted to happen. The only way to prevent this is to have a will in place that specifies who the property goes to when the owner dies.

I had another client whose wife passed away after they had been married for more than 20 years. She had two children from a previous relationship. He helped raise them, but was a very strict stepparent. The children did not like him. Her will said all her personal property went to the children on her death.

Her children gutted the house. He said it looked like she had never lived there. He did not have any pictures of her or any of her clothes. I talk to my clients about making sure that the surviving spouse has some of the personal property.

Striving for Fairness

A major decision in a second marriage is how to divide the property in a way that is fair to the spouse *and* children. If you leave it all to the spouse outright, then he or she decides whom to leave it to next. That means:

- The surviving spouse could spend it all and leave the children with nothing.

- The surviving spouse could choose to leave it to someone other than the children.

- If the surviving spouse remarries and dies without a will, the new husband or wife could have a claim to at least a portion of the estate.

- If you leave it all to the spouse for life, then the children receive nothing until the spouse passes away, by which time it could be virtually depleted.

Another choice is to leave *some* assets to the spouse and *some* to the children. One way to do this is to set your life insurance proceeds to go to the children or spouse and give different assets (such as the house) to the other. One should avoid leaving a house to the spouse with no funds to maintain it.

When It All Works Out

Here is a good example of a blended family working through touchy issues and finding an amicable solution: A woman died after a brief illness, leaving her husband of 50 years and their three adult children.

After a time of mourning, the husband married again. Although not opposed to the marriage, the children were not particularly close to their father's new wife.

Having recently lost a mother, they realized how fleeting life is and that they could be facing the loss of their father as well. They were also more aware of the complexities of settling an estate, since their mother had left all her assets to her husband—expecting that he would leave them to the children after his death. No one had thought about how this arrangement would be affected by a second marriage.

With the help of an estate planning attorney, the children tactfully approached their father. They were able, with the cooperation of the new wife, to set up the appropriate trusts to protect the interests of the children and any children they might have, as well as provide for the new wife's needs.

She was also able to provide for her own children from a previous marriage with assets she owned prior to her present marriage. With a little time, effort, and expenditure, they were able to avoid a great deal of potential expense and emotional stress at the time of either the father or his wife's death.

Protecting Minor Children

Providing for minor children from a previous marriage requires particular attention to detail. Even if those children live with you and your current spouse, your previous spouse could be awarded both custody and control of their inheritance.

If that is not your desired outcome, you should make sure appropriate arrangements and legal documents are in place. You may or may not be able to control the custody issue, but you definitely can influence the control of the gifts you give (outside of any court orders already in place).

The following are some questions to address with your estate planning attorney regarding inheritances for minor children:

- How is the successor trustee selected?
- Should the surviving spouse be the trustee?
- How will the successor trustee feel about the surviving spouse?
- How can the surviving spouse be prevented from changing the deceased spouse's beneficiaries?
- How would the children feel about the stepparent spending their inheritance?
- What is the relationship between the successor trustee and the surviving spouse and/or the children?
- How do you ensure that the succession plan will go as intended?
- How will the assets earned during the marriage be distributed?

- How should retirement plan distributions be made?

- How long should the children wait to receive their money, especially if the surviving spouse is only a few years older than the children?

By addressing these issues now, you will have greater peace of mind. This way, you can ensure that your goals, aspirations, and desires will be honored when you are no longer able to oversee them yourself.

Key Takeaways:

1. If you are anticipating remarriage, the best time to review and adjust your estate plan is before the marriage. If you have already married again, the best time is *now.*

2. The best way to avoid family stress and unintended feuds is to create a well-considered, comprehensive estate plan.

3. Consider using trusts and insurance policies to help provide fairly for different heirs.

4. Use a revocable trust to ensure you can make changes until your death or incapacity, while also making certain your wishes will be carried out afterward.

Chapter Thirteen

Sentimental Stuff

Your heirs are more likely to fight over sentimental items than anything else. There are two brothers in the city where I practice law who do not speak to each other anymore. Here is why: Each of them swears their grandmother promised *him* the grandfather clock. Even though they inherited *over a million dollars each*, they are still mad about a clock!

No one wants this sort of thing to happen in his or her family. But it does. All the time.

To prevent this kind of unfortunate and unnecessary problem, I encourage my clients to make a list of who will inherit sentimental items. I especially encourage grandparents to write down what they promise to each grandchild, because I know how easy it would be to promise the same item to more than one grandchild.

Perhaps the grandparent promises the same item to more than one person because she knows she will be gone when it is given away (and she won't have to settle the argument). On the other hand, the duplication may be the result of a failing memory. Either way, it happens. It is much kinder and more effective to make the choice now and put it in writing.

What Does Each Person Want?

It may surprise you to discover what your family members consider sentimental or valuable. After the death of her mother, one woman told me her father wanted to know which of the household furnishings and personal items she would like to have.

Without hesitation, she answered that she wanted her mother's guitar and her father's first reader, nothing more. He was shocked. He could understand the guitar (she was the only one who played), but the reader? He had no idea where it was.

She, on the other hand, knew exactly where that reader was. She had looked at the reader many times while growing up and would treasure it. He insisted that she must want more, but she did not.

It was good that he asked, because he would have tried to divide the family's possessions fairly, according to his values. As it turned out, each of his adult children truly wished for different things.

But sometimes it does not happen that way, and more than one person wants the same thing. It is best to learn this ahead of time and come to a fair decision about it. Someone may be disappointed, but it will be easier to deal with these emotions now than when they are grieving the greater loss of their parent or grandparent.

Documenting Family Stories

Family history should be preserved. It is good to write down what you know, or can discover, so it is not lost. I have had many clients tell me they wish they had a recording of the family history their parents once shared with them.

Often, they will tell me that their mother told them the history behind an item so many times that they were sick of hearing it. Now that Mom is gone, however, they can't remember the details.

By creating an audio or video recording, or writing down your memories, you can preserve your family's stories and information for future generations. It can be as simple as writing all of the stories down and placing them in a notebook to include in the division of family assets, or as elaborate as individually dividing up all of the family heirlooms and memorabilia. The memories may be written, videotaped, or audiotaped.

Even if you think your family does not have many interesting stories, ask older relatives and even your own siblings. You may be delightfully surprised at what you discover.

Try to think of any stories your grandparents or parents told you about their past, and imagine how wonderful it would be for your own grandchildren and great-grandchildren to continue telling those stories and treasuring their family heirlooms.

Next, think of your own life. Here are a few stories you might share:

- What was life like when you were younger?
- Were you raised on a farm? (Maybe your grandchildren have never even visited one.)
- Did you have fewer conveniences then?

- What did you do for entertainment? Was your first television set black-and-white, and did it have only a few channels?

- Were there school rules that would seem amusing now?

When I was a freshman in college, my history teacher had us interview our parents and grandparents. We asked them how they met, what their first job was, and where they lived as a child.

I learned so many things about my parents and grandparents that I would never have learned had she not given us that assignment. At the time, I did not see the point of it, but those tape recordings are now something I treasure.

Labeling Your History

Family pictures and letters between friends and relatives can also become treasures. This is especially true if the pictures are identified and labeled. It is sad to see old family photographs in secondhand shops or the trash because no one knows who they belong to anymore.

I know of one lady who inherited a cloth bag containing letters received by her grandmother. She also inherited family photos when an aunt passed away. From those items, she was able to locate previously unknown relatives in distant states.

She also traced relatives who fought in the Civil War, the War of 1812, and even the American Revolution.

Now, each year at Christmas, all of the younger family members receive one or more new stories to put in the family history binders she provided for them. It is easy Christmas shopping as well as an important legacy. Don't underestimate the value of your sentimental treasures.

Marking What Is Valuable

James' Uncle Fred passed away a few years ago. He collected old tractors. Fortunately, James and his dad knew someone reputable to find out the value of the tractors before selling them. Uncle Fred really enjoyed going to tractor shows and looking at tractors. It was good to make sure that he had not purchased some really valuable tractors over the years. Of course, it would have been even better   to find out that he had collected some that were surprisingly valuable.

It made me think of the different things that people collect. If you collect anything of value, leave a note to your family concerning what the items are worth, and any history you know about them. It is also a good idea to provide the name of someone to contact if they choose to sell the items.

I enjoy watching the TV series "American Pickers." It is amazing to see some of the things that look like junk to me but are deemed valuable by the pickers. If you have something that is or may be valuable and your family is possibly unaware of its worth, be sure to let them know.

I found one helpful website called *antiquehelper.com*. Looking at it, I don't think my thimble collection will go for much, but I have some really good memories of the places we visited to collect those thimbles. When I am gone, the boys will probably argue over who gets stuck with my collection. If I promise them to a grandchild, I will be sure to put it on my list.

Preserving Your Memories

Many people think of estate planning mostly in terms of preserving and passing on money and property to their families. But you have other treasures that shouldn't be overlooked when determining what you'll give to your heirs.

There may be heirlooms such as china, crystal, jewelry, a book, a musical instrument, childhood toys, etc. These things will be valued more for their meaningful connections and memories than for their monetary worth.

You also have your values, experiences, wisdom, and observations about life. When shared, these can make a world of difference to your heirs. Few of us will choose the time-consuming option of penning our memoirs. That is okay. An easier option is to create a video memoir. Just imagine how wonderful it would be to have such a gift from your ancestors.

Sample Questions for Your "Video Memoir"

You can print the sample questions below and either read them aloud or ask a trusted friend to interview you:

- Where were you born, and how did your family happen to be living there?

- Are there religious, moral, and ethical values that have guided your life, and from whom, or from what experiences, did you learn them?

- What are some of the things that make you proud of your life?

- What are some of the mistakes you've made in life, and what did you learn from them?

- What have you learned about _____ over the years?
  - living a good life
  - choosing a mate
  - marriage
  - business
  - money
  - rearing children
  - how to treat others/kindness
  - aging

- How have your religious and moral values affected how you view yourself and others?

- Tell us about your children: Name and birth order, one or two traits you appreciate and admire, what you wish for each child's future, and your special message of love for each.

- Are there traditions or rituals that have been a part of your family's life? Were these handed down or did you develop them yourself?

- Who are/were the most influential people in your life, and what is the most important thing you learned from each of them?

- What are you passionate about? Do you have causes that you contribute to or offer volunteer services?

- Name your biggest challenges in life and what you've gained from these experiences.

- What are some of the things for which you are most grateful?

- Is there anything you wish you could do over? Why?

- With regard to work or career choices, what has been the most rewarding? Does that affect what you wish for your children and/or grandchildren? If yes, how so?

  Where do you currently live and what brought you to this place?

- What are the qualities you have most appreciated in your spouse?

- Do you believe you will meet again? Or that you will still be "with" your spouse in some way?

- What do you wish for your spouse's future?

- Any expressions of love or a final farewell?

Key Takeaways:

1. Monetary value is often outclassed by sentimental value when it comes to legacies. Emotional attachment linked to memories can inflate the value of seemingly common items.

2. Make a list of the things you think your family members will value, and include the things you want them to value.

3. Ask family members to identify which of your possessions hold sentimental value for them and let them share their stories with you.

4. Decide which items you will leave to whom, and clearly identify each gift, leaving a picture or video recording if possible. You could also choose to gift the items while you are still living.

5. If more than one person chooses the same item, you will need to decide. Do not leave it unclear. This can result in disputes and hard feelings when your family is grieving.

6. Preserve your family's history by writing it down or videotaping it. If you do not feel comfortable with the task, ask for help, or you may hire someone to write your stories for you.

Chapter Fourteen

Until We Meet Again

In this book, we have discussed a number of issues pertaining to estate planning. By now, you have probably learned some things you never realized you needed to know. You may have had discussions with your family and loved ones that had never come up before. You are also aware that the most helpful estate planning attorneys are those who continually stay up to date on the laws that govern how we manage our stuff while we are living and how we pass it on to others. You should require more than these basics, however. You need your estate planning attorney to be caring as well as competent.

One especially important thing you need from a good estate planning attorney is help for your family in times of crisis. I often ask new clients to tell me who prepared their will or trust.

One of the sad things I have heard many clients say is something like, "It was some guy in Dallas or Houston," or "It was done someplace back East. He wasn't very friendly and I don't remember his name." This type of response makes me very sad. Estate planning should not be handled in such a careless and neglectful manner.

I want to have a relationship with my clients and their families, so when there is a death or disability they know *exactly* who to call. You, as the client, should feel confident that your attorney will walk you through whatever you need. I want to know my clients and their families before a crisis occurs. No one wants to deal with a stranger during difficult times.

Requesting a Review Every Three Years

A good estate planning attorney should also want to make sure your estate plan is kept current, so that it reflects your choices and meets your family's needs. Your estate plan should be reviewed (at least) every three years to make sure it still expresses your wishes.

Frequently, when I meet with a client to go over what has happened in their family, I will discover new things that need to be changed in their estate plan. For example, when a client met with me for his three-year review, I asked if there were any changes he knew of that we needed to make to his living trust.

He said there were none. Later in the interview, I asked him specific questions about what was going on in the lives of his children and grandchildren. When I got to his daughter, he said she'd been in a car wreck and had suffered a head injury. She was unable to remember numbers or handle money.

Her husband was taking great care of her, so her father was not directly responsible for her care. But the father was leaving her over

$100,000 outright, and in her present situation, she was not going to be able to manage that money.

At the very least, she would need someone to manage the funds for her. Depending on the severity of her injury, she may at some point in her life need to rely on government benefits. The money he leaves her would be safer in a trust to meet her additional expenses, without disqualifying her for those programs. A change was definitely in order.

In another three-year review meeting, I uncovered that a former son-in-law was still named executor. Now, a *former* son-in-law might still be good with accounting, but he may not be the appropriate person to handle the estate for his ex-in-laws or the legacies they leave their daughter.

I have also discovered children and grandchildren who had disabilities. These heirs with disabilities would certainly require special needs trusts. Many other issues arise in these meetings that clients are not always aware need to be addressed. These details can be easy to overlook in the course of daily living, but they are quickly apparent to a good estate planning attorney.

Questions to Revisit with Your Estate Planning Attorney

Once you create an estate plan, it is very easy to just file it away and assume everything is covered for every possible future situation. It would be wise to review your current plan carefully and include your estate planning attorney in the process. Here are some questions to consider:

- * Does your trust or will protect the assets your beneficiaries inherit against divorce, lawsuits, and creditors?
- * Do we need to discuss protecting your assets in the event that you need to go into a nursing home?
- * Who will take care of your children if you can't?
- * If your will or trust was prepared when the children were young, are their needs different now that they are grown?
- * If you have retirement accounts totaling more than $200,000, have you set up a Retirement Plan Trust to protect those accounts?
- Are all your assets in the trust name? Have you recently purchased any assets that are not in the trust name?
- Did you purchase any life insurance or annuities? If so, are the beneficiaries properly designated?
- Did you review or update your estate plan to account for the changes to the state and federal laws?
- Have you updated your trust and advance health-care directive to account for the HIPAA medical information act ("Privacy Laws")?
- Have there been any changes in your family?
- Do you want to change the people named as executor and trustee?
- Do you want to change any of the beneficiaries or how they receive property?

Of course, we would all rather enjoy our time and resources with our families, with no thought of possible unfortunate changes. Some changes are predictable, though we may not know how soon they may occur. Other changes are not necessarily predictable, but they certainly can happen. In every case, it is good to be prepared for as many situations as possible. If you live in an area where hurricanes are frequent, it makes sense to have an evacuation plan in place. If you live where the temperature is very cold, you make sure you have a good heating system and backup in case it fails. If you live in Texas, you make sure you have good air-conditioning and have it serviced regularly!

We always hope for the best, but we should also plan to prevent the worst whenever we can.

Author's Note:

If I created your will or trust and we have not seen you in over three years, please give my office a call to schedule your free consultation to review your estate plan. When I design an estate plan for my clients, I discuss the importance of reviewing that plan every three years. A lot can change in a few years and sometimes people forget the review. I would love to sit down with you and your family (at no charge) to discuss what has changed since you prepared the will or trust. If you are not my client, find out how your estate planning attorney handles the three-year review. In either case, schedule an appointment to review your plan.

Appendix I

The Pros and Cons of Guardianships

Guardianships come in various shapes and sizes, and are definitely not one-size-fits-all. Some things they all have in common are:

1) Someone (the Guardian) takes on some portion of another person's decision-making responsibilities.

2) Someone (the Ward) loses some decision-making authority.

There are some very good reasons why this must happen in certain cases, and others why it should happen only when absolutely necessary. For instance, an adult may have some permanent disability rendering him or her unable to make certain decisions regarding their health, safety, or finances.

They may be perfectly able to handle their own medical decisions, maintain adequate living conditions, and get adequate nutrition, but be unable to manage their finances. This does not just mean making foolish spending decisions. (That would put many of us in need of guardians!) It may simply mean that the person is not able to do simple math, or comprehend monetary units or values. Even in this situation, the person may be able to rely on a trustworthy individual (often a relative) or an agency to manage their money. If such assistance is not available or the person's disability makes them a target for fraud or abuse, a guardianship may be needed.

In another situation, a person may be able to handle their finances appropriately, and yet be unable to manage their living conditions or basic health needs. Again, agencies and programs are often able to provide adequate support, and guardianship may be avoided.

This sometimes happens when aging or illness results in diminished abilities. Someone realizes that the person needs help, but can't provide it, or perhaps help is refused. A social worker or health care provider may be able to mediate or assist with finding help that is acceptable to the individual. If all else fails, it may be necessary to seek guardianship of the person.

Of course, a person may be disabled in a way that requires guardianship in all areas. Regardless of the type of guardianship needed, the legal process must be followed.

Establishing a Guardianship

To establish a guardianship, a petition must be filed in the Probate Court. Any interested person may file such a petition, even if that person does not personally want to be appointed guardian.

The court must then determine if the individual named in the petition is, in fact, incapacitated in a way that necessitates a guardian.

That individual is referred to in the legal proceeding as the "proposed ward." This requires several actions:

- Notice must be sent to the proposed ward informing them that guardianship is being sought.

- An "attorney *ad litem*" must be appointed by the court to provide legal representation for the proposed ward. The attorney *ad litem*'s role is to determine the desire of the proposed ward and present all available legal arguments to the court. He or she must also attempt to obtain the proposed ward's desired outcome as to whether a guardianship will be created, the extent of any guardianship, and, if one is created, who the guardian will be.

- A "guardian *ad litem*" may also be appointed by the court to investigate the facts and submit a report to the court with recommendations regarding the "best interests" of the proposed ward (which are not always consistent with the desires of the proposed ward whom the attorney *ad litem* must advocate).

- The applicant must also submit a statement from a physician.

- A proposed guardian must be identified and vetted. If this is an individual who is not a professional guardian, some training may be required. In a few circumstances, the court may waive the training, but usually it must be completed. The purpose of such training is to be sure the guardian understands what the court expects of them. There are laws to be followed and reports to be submitted. If no relative or friend is suggested, a professional guardian may be proposed.

- The court must then hold a hearing. The person who has been identified as incapacitated may object at the hearing. That person may present his or her own evidence and even reports from a doctor or psychologist. This might be unusual, but nothing may be assumed until all facts are presented. If the court decides that a guardian is needed and that the proposed guardian is suitable, the guardianship will be issued. Appropriate documents are then created that identify the ward, the guardian, and the specific limitations and authorities of the guardian.

As you can see, this is not a matter that is taken lightly by our courts. Nor is it something that should be considered embarrassing, bad, or wrong. Sometimes it is a necessity, and it must be treated with the seriousness and respect it deserves.

Things a Guardian Can't Do

Even when a guardianship is issued, there are some decisions a guardian may not make. For example, the guardian can't consent to committing the ward to an inpatient psychiatric facility, nor can the guardian sign a Do Not Resuscitate Order (DNR) for an incapacitated person. These actions, if needed, would have to be handled as involuntary and the court would have to make the decision.

The guardian must also make decisions based on the ward's values and preferences, if known. It should always be the goal to respect the opinions and choices of the individual, regardless of his or her current incapacity.

Despite all of the safeguards, there have been abuses. Appointed guardians have managed to isolate their wards from caring family, diverted funds for their own use, and neglected to provide necessary care and even medical attention.

There have been some notable cases, including one report of a pastor who managed to be appointed guardian of the estates of multiple parishioners. He was able to gain control of huge amounts of money and use them for his own gain. While this was exceptional enough to make headlines, it does point out the need to be cautious.

Alternatives to Guardianships

Guardianships are not always the right answer. Here are several alternatives to consider, depending on each situation:

- While the person still has capacity, he or she can create documents that may remove the need for a guardian in the future. For instance, "guardian of the estate" can be avoided by creating a living trust. (Once a person has lost their capacity, however, they can no longer create a living trust and guardianship may be the only option.)

-

- Less restrictive alternatives, such as supported decision-making agreements, may also be possible if the incapacitated person has a relative or other person who can help explain choices and make decisions.

- While the person still has capacity, he or she can identify someone to help manage money, including paying bills.

- A joint checking account may be set up, allowing another person to assist in managing funds for the person who needs help.

- A "representative payee" can request government benefits for the incapacitated person and open a bank account for that person.

- A person can name someone to make health care decisions for him or her.

- There are a number of support services for people with disabilities that make it possible for them to manage their lives independently. These include home health care, Meals on Wheels, transportation services, emergency call devices, and other special services for people with disabilities.

- Your local area agency on aging for people sixty and older, their families, and other caregivers (such as DADS) can assist with identifying a myriad of services that may give a person the support they need without guardianship.

The best way to avoid the need for guardianship is through preventive steps that can be taken by a person before they become disabled. Your estate planning attorney can assist with crafting the necessary documents, which include health-care durable powers of attorney, durable financial powers of attorney, and revocable trusts.

Key Takeaways:

1. There are several types of Adult Guardianships:
   a) Guardian of the person
   b) Guardian of the estate
   c) Guardian of the person and the estate

2 All guardianships are ordered by the court.

3 All authorities given to the appointed guardian are expressly stated.

4 Because the rights given to the guardian are taken away from the ward, guardianships are serious matters and should be avoided when other less restrictive means can be used.

5 To avoid the necessity of guardianship in our own futures, we can work with an estate planning attorney to set up powers of attorney and trusts. This allows us to decide who will act for us in the event of temporary or permanent incapacity.

6 Guardianships may be unavoidable in certain situations, such as those in which an individual loses capacity prior to signing

the types of documents discussed herein or in situations in which an individual is highly susceptible to financial and/or personal exploitation.

Appendix II

Choosing an Executor or Trustee

Whether your estate is large or small, simple or complex, you will want to choose wisely who will handle the affairs of your estate when the time comes to pass it on.

Many people think of it as an honor to be chosen, while others view it as an opportunity to have power. For example, a husband might resent having his wife choose someone other than him if he is used to handling the family finances. Or the wife might resent having a business partner or relative "in charge" if she thinks it ought to be her right. Siblings might feel slighted if another is chosen.

While some people consider it an honor to be trusted and chosen as executor, it can also take a lot of time and effort. If the affairs of the estate are well organized and easily accessible, the job is easier. If the estate is large, or relationships between the heirs are not harmonious, the job can be much harder.

Executor and Trustee Expectations

The best way to begin the task of choosing who will act on your behalf is to think about the tasks they will need to perform. Here is a list of what is usually expected of the executor:

- Determine what assets are in the estate. This includes bank accounts, physical property (such as a home, cars, and vacation or investment property), insurance policies, retirement funds, and business holdings.

- Determine who the heirs are and get detailed contact information for each. If the executor is not an attorney, they will probably need to secure legal help to begin the probate process. If you have an attorney who is your estate planning attorney, be sure to leave that person's contact information for your executor. This will make the process much smoother.

- Pay any bills owed, including any funeral expenses.

- File necessary tax reports and pay taxes.

- Distribute the estate to beneficiaries according to the will.

Looking at this list, you can already narrow your choices by considering who would have the necessary time and ability to take on such a task. It does not have to be someone who already knows how to do all of these jobs. But it does need to be someone who can figure out which matters to tackle on their own and which ones will require help. It should be someone you know to be honest, ethical, and detail-oriented.

If a family member has the necessary character, skills, and temperament, he or she may be a good choice and will lessen your out-of-pocket expenses. If, however, there are problems between the heirs, appointing someone outside the family may be advisable. This is also true if there are troublesome or complex business matters involved.

It is not necessary for the executor to have business or legal expertise, but sometimes it is just the smart thing to do if you know that experience will be necessary to deal with the estate.

With the help of your estate planning attorney, evaluate who will be the best choice for your estate's management. Once you decide, be sure to choose an alternate as well.

Also, be sure to communicate with the person, agency, or institution you choose. Some institutions, like banks, will only handle estates worth a certain amount of money. Make sure your estate qualifies. If you are naming an individual, talk with him or her to see if they are willing and available. Be sure to explain fully what would be expected of them. For any number of reasons, that person may refuse to serve, but you would much rather know now if they are willing.

You should also let your heirs know what you have set up. This will make it less likely that anyone will be further disturbed at a time when they are grieving.

Don't forget to look at your estate plan—including your choice of executor and/or trustee—at least every three years, or when something important changes.

Appendix III

What Should You Look for in an Estate Planning Attorney?

When one looks for an estate planning attorney, people may do an Internet search, talk to attorneys who have done other work for them, or ask friends. Despite how basic a will preparation may seem, no one should have "just anybody" draft one for them. Finding the right attorney to plan your estate is crucial, and you need to carefully vet any attorney you hire to handle something as important as your family and your estate. So before you schedule that initial consultation, be sure to ask and answer the following questions about your prospective lawyer.

Is the attorney's primary focus on estate planning?

An attorney whose practice is broad but includes simple estate planning and probate matters might not recognize issues that need to be addressed in your estate plan. On the other hand, an attorney whose primary focus is on estate planning will recognize issues and provide the best protection for your family and situation.

How many years of experience does the attorney have?

The more years of experience the attorney has, the more the attorney will have had the opportunity to see their essential estate planning documents in action when a client becomes disabled or dies. The wills, trusts, powers of attorney, and health care documents used by attorneys who have been in business for a while have been revised and tweaked to deal with the everyday situations that their clients encounter. This will give you peace of mind, knowing that the documents they prepare for you will work when they are needed.

Does the attorney assist clients with properly funding their assets into a revocable living trust?

Many attorneys create beautiful estate plans for their clients but then fail to assist them with the next important step: funding the revocable living trust. A well-drafted trust will be virtually useless immediately after you die if your assets are not titled in the name of the trust while you are still alive. A good firm will provide you with comprehensive written instructions. Still, others will merely mention the importance of funding but fail to give you any guidance whatsoever.

Does the attorney charge a fixed price or an hourly rate for providing estate planning and other services?

This is an important question to ask so that you won't be surprised by hidden fees and costs. It is better to work with an attorney who charges a fixed price. This will give you the peace of mind of knowing that the fixed price is all that you'll be required to pay.

Ask yourself: "Can I see myself working closely with this attorney?"

Even if the prospective attorney answers all of the other questions to your satisfaction, this is the most important question that you need to ask yourself. If you are not comfortable with the attorney, then chances are you won't be happy with the attorney's work. But don't be alarmed; it is better to determine this sooner rather than later. Simply move on until you find an attorney you feel comfortable enough with to trust with your family's well-being.

Appendix IV

Preventing Caregiver Burnout

Caregivers have an incredible responsibility—one that many caring people choose to do for a living. But others are unexpectedly thrust into this role unprepared.

As such, many caregivers can become afflicted with a real condition known as caregiver burnout, which is a state of physical, emotional, and mental exhaustion that can change the caregiver's attitude from positive to negative.

Burnout most often occurs when caregivers are not able to get the help they need, or if they try to do more than they can handle, either physically or financially. Burned-out caregivers may be fatigued, stressed, anxious, and depressed. Many also have accompanying feelings of guilt if they spend time for themselves instead of caring for their loved ones.

Symptoms of Caregiver Burnout

If you or someone in your family serves as a primary caregiver, here are some signs that indicate you may be overextending yourself:

- Withdrawal from friends and family
- Loss of interest in activities

- Feelings of hopelessness and helplessness

- Changes in appetite and/or weight

- Sleep pattern changes

- Becoming sick

- Physical and emotional exhaustion

- Unusual irritability

Avoiding Caregiver Burnout

There are many ways to prevent caregiver burnout. The most important one is to be *realistic* by setting reachable goals, understanding that you may need help, and asking for what you need.

Also, be realistic about your loved one's illness—especially with progressive diseases such as Parkinson's, Alzheimer's, and terminal cancer. And don't forget to be realistic about your own limitations too.

Next, remember to take care of yourself. Find someone to talk to about your feelings and frustrations, such as a professional counselor or a caregiver support group. And always set aside at least an hour or two a day *for yourself.* Don't think of it as being selfish, because in reality, it is a necessity.

In addition, understand that your feelings of frustration are normal. They do not make you a bad person. Bottling your emotions is much more difficult than venting to someone supportive who understands.

What if You Have Caregiver Burnout or Know Someone Else Who Does?

If you or someone you know is a caregiver and is already suffering from stress and depression, seek medical attention as soon as possible. Both stress and depression are treatable.

Your next steps would be to contact outside resources for assistance. These can include home health services, adult day care, private care aides, professional caregivers, caregiver support services, and nursing homes or assisted living facilities.

Appendix V

Challenges and Choices for Widows/Widowers

There are few things in life more challenging than dealing with all the choices one must make after the death of a spouse. Often, the early days are filled with grief and shock, as well as an overwhelming number of decisions that must be made.

In an ideal situation, a well-crafted estate plan would be in place that would minimize the number of immediate actions needed.

In any case, the surviving spouse will also receive much advice, some from loving, well-meaning friends and family. But there are others who may seek to take advantage of the situation. In this section we will cover things you must do immediately, and other matters that you can—and should—delay.

Sharing Your Burden

The following are items that can make this process a little easier during one of the hardest times in your life. The key is to *not* take every task on yourself. Here is what you should do immediately:

- *Rely on your support system.* This may include close friends, family, ministers, and counselors for emotional and spiritual support.

- *Depend on trusted professionals for financial and business matters.* Relying on friends to advise you in these areas may lead to costly mistakes. Something that worked well for a friend five years ago may not work well for you now. Professionals are constantly updating their information to include the latest laws and constantly changing financial realities.

- *Address your immediate financial situation.* Determine your resources and necessary expenditures. Keep recurring expenses such as credit card payments, house and car payments, and taxes current to avoid late charges and damage to your credit rating. You must also immediately deal with your bank to determine your liquid assets. There may be unexpected changes. The bank may have frozen your accounts if they are not jointly owned. The Social Security Administration may reclaim your spouse's most recent Social Security deposit.

- *Gather and organize documents.* These include: birth, marriage and divorce certificates, titles to cars, real estate, statements for checking, savings, and brokerage accounts, retirement accounts, and insurance policies.

Stuff You Can Deal with Later

Even after you have weathered the overwhelming task of getting through those first few months, there will be more decisions to be made. Many of those can wait and often *should* wait.

Prioritize these decisions to determine which ones need attention first and which ones you can address later:

- Decide if you want to remain in your home or sell it and relocate.

- Review investments and determine if anything needs to change.

- Update your estate plans, budget for your new circumstances, and determine if you want to make changes in your lifestyle or activities.

No matter how many decisions or changes you face, you will handle them better with appropriate and plentiful support. Having the right people and plans in place before your spouse passes away will help more than anything else.

It helps to find activities to occupy your time. Would you find you have more time to spend with grandchildren? Might you find additional purpose and meaning through volunteer work? Is there something you always wanted to do but have not yet done?

Appendix VI

Outsmarting Sibling Rivalry

We often think of protecting our assets from heavy taxes, liability suits, and even divorce. But one of the most likely (and often overlooked) threats is sibling rivalry.

Many parents expect sibling rivalry to fade away like other phases of childhood, to be replaced by family love and harmony. That can happen in many cases, but it frequently stays firmly in place.

When it comes to estate settlements, sibling rivalry can create serious problems. Should one or more of the children choose to challenge a will, the cost of litigation can be very high. Not to mention, the damage to relationships that can endure for generations.

Planning for Peace

Fortunately, there is much you can do to assure a positive outcome for your family. Plans that are carefully crafted prevent many problems—whether your children are rivals or best friends.

The first step is to avoid surprises. Keep in mind that estate settlement issues arise when people are experiencing grief and trying to cope with loss. When emotions run high, we are less likely to be logical or even cooperative.

If one sibling is disappointed, it will not matter if their expectation is reasonable or not. It will only matter that they are dealing with this additional experience of loss at a very difficult time.

Assigning Sentimental Items

When it comes to sentimental items, start by letting your children tell you what is important to them. Parents are often surprised to learn the value of "that old thing" to one of their children. If more than one child wants the same item, you may have to get creative about choosing, or let them assist you in finding a fair way to determine who will inherit the item.

If one sibling selects something of much greater monetary value, you may decide to alter your estate plan to give the others more money or more items to create a more equal distribution.

There may be reasons for unequal distribution of assets and those reasons should be made clear ahead of time. For example, you may have already given or loaned money to one sibling and not the other. Be sure to account for this and explain whether you are adjusting the distribution accordingly or not.

In other situations, one sibling may spend time and effort caring for elderly or disabled parents while another does not. The "caregiver" sibling may even have control of the parents' money and/or medical decisions.

Each of the siblings is sure to have an opinion about what is fair. You may be wise to prepare for such a possibility.

An experienced estate planning lawyer can help you create the appropriate documents that will be fair *and* protect the interests of both the caregiver and other siblings.

Thinking Through Personality Conflicts

Conflict between siblings is not always about money or sentimental things. It is also likely to be about who will be in charge.

Some people choose an adult child as executor or trustee. While that child may obviously have more of the necessary skills for the task, it may cause discord between the siblings. Making two or more siblings co-executors or co-trustees, however, is not helpful if they don't agree on how things should be handled.

The same is true in choosing who will plan the funeral. Siblings often differ in matters of spending, and even in their perceptions of what their parent would want for their memorial.

One child may want something small and intimate, while another can't imagine *not* including all their parent's friends.

One child may judge how loved their mother was by counting the flower arrangements sent. Another may be sure their mother would prefer donations made in her memory to a favorite charity.

Such differences may seem petty, but they can feel important in the midst of grief. Making prior arrangements for your memorial and burial assures your children that your wishes are being respected. Important decisions don't have to be debated, and your children will be free to experience grief and healing in their own way.

You love your children and you hope you can count on them to love each other and treat each other with kindness and generosity. Wise planning can make it easier for them to do as you wish. The estate planning attorneys at Leigh Hilton P.L.L.C. take care to create plans that have the best chance of turning out well. We are trained to anticipate and prevent problems between heirs. We will also help communicate your wishes to your families so that issues can be identified and resolved. We can't offer a cure for sibling rivalry, but we can deal with it effectively, thereby ensuring that your estate will be settled as smoothly and peacefully as you wish it to be.

Appendix VII

Estate Planning for Pets

We have all heard about people who leave fortunes to their pets. Some people are critical about how those millions could have been put to better use. Others regard their own pets as beloved members of the family, and completely understand.

Even if you don't plan on leaving money to your pet, you should think about how your pet will be cared for if you pass away or become disabled. Agreements from family members or friends are good, but life happens. It is possible that changes in their own circumstances may prevent them from honoring their commitment.

Including your pet (and instructions for their care) in a will may not be sufficient. There can be delays in probating the will, leaving a gap in the pet's care. Furthermore, a will can't protect your pets if you are disabled.

Fortunately, there are legal documents that are both flexible and enforceable for proper pet estate planning. You can still mention your pet in your will, but other steps should be taken as well. It would be better to have a living trust that includes provisions for your pet's care. The trustee of your trust can immediately assume care of your pets without the delay of probate.

How Pet Estate Planning Works

In either a will or a living trust, you can create a pet trust. This will allow you to name a trustee who will be able to manage funds for the pet's care. This need not be the same person who will be the pet's caregiver. You can also name an alternate in the event your first choice can't serve at the time.

If the funds are managed wisely, they may be sufficient to care generously for your pet during its lifetime and still allow for a charitable gift later.

One of the most important benefits of the living trust is that it leaves you in charge as long as you are able. It becomes effective, however, when you are disabled or deceased. In the event of disability, you can even specify that your pet will remain with you even if you are in a nursing home or long-term care facility. (Note: it is a good idea to research facilities in your area to identify the ones that allow and even encourage pets.)

Creating a Letter of Intent

Another step would be to create a letter of intent for your pet's caregiver. While this is not legally enforceable, it is an invaluable tool to help those you have entrusted with your pet's care. You can be as creative and expressive with this as you like. Here are some provisions it should include:

- Your pet's legal name and nickname
- Pedigree information, if applicable
- Names and contact information for the veterinarian and groomer
- Information regarding the pet trust, caregiver, and trustee
- Shot records and schedule of care
- Dietary needs and preferences
- Favorite toys, walking routes, and treats
- Daily schedule
- Where your pet sleeps
- Anything else that will help ensure your pet's comfort and health

In the event that you have more than one pet, provide all of the above information for each one. You can also specify that two or more pets should stay together.

Remember to provide copies of all documents and instructions to everyone concerned: the caregiver, the trustee, the vet, the groomer, and the estate planning lawyer. This will make it much easier for everyone to cooperate on behalf of your pet.

Many pet owners find it hard to describe how much love and affection exists between them. For that reason, a growing number of people are providing for their pets as well as their families in their estate plans.

At our firm, we are happy to encourage and support this sentiment with carefully drawn documents worthy of those relationships. If you are not sure your pets are protected in your current estate plan, call us to discuss how we can help to fill that need.

Appendix VIII

Why Online Wills Are a Huge Mistake

There are several websites that offer the creation of legal documents, such as wills, trusts, and business creation documents, for a far cheaper price than it would cost to hire an attorney. Hiring an attorney to draft your will or trust is expensive, and no estate planning attorney will tell you otherwise. However, they will tell you that it is worth it, because as great as these online legal services seem, they truly are too good to be true.

Saving money now with one of these services could end up costing you and your family far more money down the road than it would have cost you to hire an estate planning attorney to get it right the first time.

The Pitfalls of Online Planning

No matter what these online services promote, they are not law firms. They are not even overseen by lawyers, so they can't give legal advice. All these services do is plug your information into generic forms. Approximately 80% of wills created online end up with a problem when their families go to probate them. These problems can cost the family thousands more than a properly drafted will prepared by an attorney. In the past year, we have probated eight wills that were created online that caused their families problems. Several of these were written to require a dependent administration, which is dramatically more expensive.

They do not customize your will or trust for your specific needs. If you make a mistake, they can't stop you or even warn you, as that would be giving legal advice. And because they can't give legal advice, these services typically design their forms as one-size-fits-all. With that in mind, here are some things you can't do with online planning services:

- You can't set up a special needs trust that guarantees your child can still claim government benefits.

- You can't set up a will or a trust with specific instructions for how your assets should be handled.

- You can't guarantee that anything you put in your will or trust is legally viable.

- You can't guarantee what your draft specifies will hold up in a court of law.

- You can't receive legal advice or learn about possible opportunities or errors.

All an online service *can* do is save you money. But how much money have you really saved if your will or trust has an egregious error that must be fixed during a court proceeding? Your family could end up spending your entire estate trying to clean up the mess.

Appendix IX

Steps to Take After Losing a Loved One

After you lose a loved one, the last thing you want to worry about is taking care of his or her estate. The good news is most things can wait a few months before needing attention.

Immediate Action Required

Here are a few items that will need immediate attention:

1. Notify Social Security.

If your loved one was receiving Social Security checks, Social Security must be notified of his or her death. You can call their office at 800-772-1213 or visit their website at socialsecurity.gov and notify them. Most likely, all payments will stop or be frozen by the bank if they are directly deposited.

2. Keep property safe from theft.

Remove all valuables from the decedent's home and take extra steps to secure the house from theft or vandalism. Keep a list of any items you do remove, including where you moved them. If you do not live in the house, put a stop on all incoming mail.

3. Address outstanding debt.

When someone dies, their debt does not die with them. Before the estate can be distributed, all outstanding debt must be addressed. It is also a good idea to notify the decedent's credit card companies, and cancel their cards in writing. Many creditors will offer an extension until you have time to gather the assets. Do not allow creditors to pressure you into paying before you have a chance to assess all the debts owed by the estate.

Items That Can Wait

Fortunately, other things can wait a few months. Estate distribution is laden with paperwork as well as very strict deadlines, and if any mistakes are made—or steps missed—it can cause financial difficulties and delays for everyone involved.

Here are the steps you should take as the estate administrator to avoid costly mistakes:

1. **List all property and documents.**

There is no guarantee your loved one has everything in an easy-to-find place. Or maybe they do, but things are not up to date. Documents you'll need to locate are:

- Real estate information, including any property that is business-related or used for vacation
- Bank accounts
- Retirement accounts
- Safe deposit boxes

- Stocks and bonds
- Certified copies of the decedent's birth certificate, death certificate, and marriage certificate (if any)
- Divorce decrees from all previous marriages (if any)
- Will or trust documents
- Insurance policies
- Social Security numbers (both yours and the decedent's)
- Credit card numbers and statements
- Real estate deeds
- Tax return from previous year

1. Open claims for insurance benefits.

Gather the decedent's insurance policies and notify companies of the policyholder's death. Be prepared with the policy number and death certificate so you can make any claims in regard to health insurance, life insurance, and any private retirement accounts. All proceeds from the policies will automatically be sent to whomever is named beneficiary.

2. Research additional benefits from former employers.

Contact the human resources department at the decedent's place of employment and ask if they offer death benefits to the surviving spouse or family. Sometimes employers offer these benefits to former employees, so contact all of the decedent's former employers if possible. Be sure to also ask about the decedent's 401(k) accounts, pensions, or stock options.

3. Contact an estate planning attorney.

Now that you have all the paperwork gathered and agencies notified, it is time to bring on an experienced estate planning attorney to help you with the rest of the estate administration.

From this point forward, you're in the most time-consuming, confusing, and potentially costly portion of administering an estate. An attorney will doubly ensure that no mistakes are made and all deadlines are met.

It may sound more expensive to hire an attorney than it is to handle the probate yourself, but remember, hiring an attorney is far cheaper than paying to fix mistakes and missed deadlines. At this point, you are undoubtedly mentally exhausted, so why not let a professional take the reins from here?

Appendix X

Important Definitions

ABLE Accounts: Achieving a Better Life Experience (ABLE) accounts allow the families of disabled young people to set aside money for their care in a way that earns special tax benefits. ABLE accounts work much like the so-called 529 accounts that families use to save money for education. In fact, an ABLE account is really a special kind of 529. Here are two requirements your family member must meet prior to opening an ABLE account:

1. *Have a qualifying disability* – must either be eligible for SSI/SSDI or be able to self-certify that they meet certain disability standards.

2. *Disability started before age 26* – need not be formally diagnosed with the disability but must be able to prove disability before age 26.

Guardian of the Estate: A guardian of the estate attends to the financial affairs of the ward and is tasked with managing, protecting, preserving, and disposing of the ward's estate in accordance with the law.

And, like the guardian of the person, the guardian of the estate is charged with furthering the ward's best interests.

The guardian of the estate has the obligation to use the assets of the estate to provide for the care and maintenance of the ward, or a person whom the ward is legally bound to support. The guardian of the estate generally is granted the authority to make decisions regarding the ward's property and estate as if he or she were the owner, but state law may prescribe some limits.

For example, some states do not permit a guardian of the estate to execute a will on the ward's behalf. State law may allow (or disallow) a guardian of the estate to transfer assets for particular reasons, such as to be eligible for Medicaid.

Guardian of the Person: A guardian of the person is authorized to make decisions involving the life and person of the ward, including health care decisions and place of residence.

The guardian is tasked with arranging appropriate personal care, maintenance, and support for the ward, as well as medical, dental, and other necessary treatments. State law establishes limits on the court-appointed guardian's authority, and prior court approval may be required for certain decisions.

For example, the guardian generally has the authority to decide the ward's place of residence, but some states will not permit the guardian to move the ward to a nursing home without prior court approval.

A guardian's right to authorize major medical treatment may also be circumscribed by state law. The actions of a guardian of the person must consistently be in the ward's best interests.

In-Kind Support and Maintenance: In-kind support and maintenance is simply food or shelter that somebody else provides for you. The Social Security Administration counts in-kind support and maintenance as income when we figure the amount of a client's SSI benefits. For example, if someone helps pay your rent, mortgage, food, or utilities, this reduces the amount of SSI benefits.

Medicaid: Medicaid provides health coverage to millions of Americans, including eligible low-income adults, children, pregnant women, elderly adults and people with disabilities. Medicaid is administered by states, according to federal requirements. The program is funded jointly by states and the federal government.

Medicare: Medicare is the federal health insurance program for:

- People who are 65 or older

- Certain younger people with disabilities

- People with end-stage renal disease (permanent kidney failure requiring dialysis or a transplant, sometimes called ESRD)

Qualified Disability Expenses: These include education, housing, employment support, health, transportation, and other life necessities.

Section 8 Housing: Section 8 of the Housing Act of 1937, often called Section 8, authorizes the payment of rental housing assistance to private landlords on behalf of approximately 4.8 million low-income households (as of 2008) in the United States.

Special Needs Trust or Supplemental-Needs Trust: These refer to the same type of trust. A third-party special needs trust or supplemental needs trust is the typical type of trust used to benefit a person with special needs. Commonly, family members create a trust for a loved one with special needs and leave property in the trust through their estate plan.

SSDI: Social Security Disability Insurance is funded through payroll taxes. SSDI recipients are considered "insured" because they have worked for a certain number of years and have made contributions to the Social Security trust fund in the form of FICA Social Security taxes. SSDI candidates must be younger than 65 and have earned a certain number of "work credits."

After receiving SSDI for two years, a disabled person will become eligible for Medicare. Under SSDI, a disabled person's spouse and children dependents are eligible to receive partial dependent benefits, called auxiliary benefits.

However, only adults over the age of 18 can receive the SSDI disability benefit. There is a five-month waiting period for benefits, meaning that the SSA won't pay you benefits for the first five months after you become disabled. The amount of the monthly benefit after the waiting period depends on your earnings record, much like the Social

Security retirement benefit. The average payment for 2020 was $1,258 per month.

SSI: Supplemental Security Income is a program that is strictly needs-based and is funded by general fund taxes (not from the Social Security trust fund). SSI is called a "means-tested program," meaning it has nothing to do with work history, but strictly with financial need.

To meet the SSI income requirements, you must have less than $2,000 in assets (or $3,000 for a couple) and a very limited income. Disabled people who are eligible under the income requirements for SSI are also able to receive Medicaid in their state of residence.

Most people who qualify for SSI will also qualify for food stamps, and the amount an eligible person will receive is dependent on where they live and the amount of regular, monthly income they have. As of 2020, the maximum SSI will pay is $783 per month.

Trust: A legal entity created by a party (the trustor) through which a second party (the trustee) holds the right to manage the trustor's assets or property for the benefit of a third party (the beneficiary). The four main types of trusts are:

1. Living trust – created by the trustor while he or she is alive.
2. Testamentary trust – established through a will and which comes into effect (is created) when the trustor dies.
3. Revocable trust – can be modified or terminated by the trustor after its creation.

4. Irrevocable trust – can't be modified or terminated by the trustor after its creation.

Will: A legal document containing instructions as to what should be done with one's money and property after one's death.

Appendix XI

Waiver Interest Lists

Community Living Assistance and Support Services (CLASS): Provides home and community-based support to children and adults with functional limitations. There are more than 200 related conditions, such as cerebral palsy and spina bifida. The related condition must have occurred before the child was age 22.

https://www.navigatelifetexas.org/en/insurance-financial-help/communityliving-assistance-and-support-services-class

Deaf Blind with Multiple Disabilities (DBMD): Provides services for children and adults who are deaf-blind or have a related condition that leads to deaf-blindness, and who have another disability.

https://www.navigatelifetexas.org/en/insurance-financial-help/deaf-blindwith-multiple-disabilities-dbmd

Home and Community-Based Services (HCS): Provides services and support to children and adults with an intellectual disability (ID) or a related condition, who live with their families, in their own homes, or in small group homes with no more than four people. The HCS program includes: residential services, adaptive aids, day habilitation (help with development of basic life skills), minor home modifications, nursing, respite, professional therapies, supported employment, and other services.

https://www.navigatelifetexas.org/en/insurance-financial-help/home-andcommunity-based-services-hcs

Medically Dependent Children Program (MDCP): Provides services to children and adults age 20 and younger who are medically fragile, as an alternative to receiving services in a nursing facility. MDCP services include: respite, adaptive aids, employment assistance, flexible family supports (services that support a person's basic daily activities like bathing, dressing, and preparing meals), and minor home modifications.

https://www.navigatelifetexas.org/en/insurance-financial-help/medicallydependent-children-program-mdcp

STAR+PLUS Home and Community-Based Services (HCBS): Provides services to adults over the age of 21, to keep them in their community and not in a nursing home facility.

https://www.navigatelifetexas.org/en/insurance-financial-help/starplushome-and-community-based-services-hcbs

Texas Home Living (TXHML): Provides services to children and adults with an intellectual disability (ID) or a related condition who live in their own home or their family's home. Services in the TxHmL program include: adaptive aids, behavioral support, community support, day habilitation (help with development of basic life skills), employment assistance, minor home modifications, nursing, respite, professional therapies, and supported employment.

https://www.navigatelifetexas.org/en/insurance-financial-help/texas-homeliving-

txhml

Youth Empowerment Services (YES): Provides home and community-based

services to children under the age of 19 who otherwise would need

psychiatric inpatient care or whose parents would turn to state custody

for care.

https://hhs.texas.gov/services/mental-health-substance-use/childrens-mental-health/yes-waiver

Appendix XII

Contact Information for Federal Agencies

Social Security Administration............................... 800.772.1213
www.SSA.gov
US Department of Veterans Affairs........................ 800.827.1000
www.VA.gov
Medicare... 800.633.4227
www.Medicare.gov
Medicaid... 877.267.2323
www.Medicaid.gov
www.cms.hhs.gov/home/medicaid.asp

Appendix XIII

Frequently Asked Questions

What is estate planning?

Estate planning involves putting your affairs in order to maximize the benefits your assets can provide to you during your lifetime (and to those you desire to benefit from them after your death).

Can I create my own estate plan?

Estate planning is more than just creating documents. It also involves understanding the big picture and how legal documents will work with your assets when they are needed.

Do I need an estate plan if I hold all my assets jointly with another person?

Honestly, this is one of the worst ways to plan your estate. Here is how it can get complicated:

- If the assets are held jointly and one of the owners dies, the assets will go to the surviving owner(s). The assets do not go to the deceased owner's children.

- It does not avoid probate, it just delays it until the last owner's death.

- It may cause the application of estate, gift, and capital gains taxes.

- It is subject to the creditors of all owners.

- It will result in the transfer of the property to the joint owner when one owner dies, even if that was not intended.

- Also, if any of the owners applies for Medicaid, the entire account will be considered his or hers and may put them over the asset limit.

Can I just put my adult child on my bank accounts and the deed to my house? Would that avoid probate and inheritance taxes?

Unfortunately, probate and inheritance taxes may not be the most important things to avoid. If your child were to have an accident resulting in a judgment against them, your bank account could be used to settle the claim.

That could also happen if unexpected changes in employment resulted in credit problems. And if the child on your account is involved in a divorce, their spouse could claim a right to your assets.

Another problem could arise if you have more than one child. In the event of your incapacity or death, only one child on your bank account or deed to your home would receive the assets, no matter what your will says. Designated beneficiaries on accounts take precedence over wills.

When should an estate plan be reviewed?

If you already have an estate plan, it should not be considered permanent. Conditions, as well as your desires, may change. Estate plans should be reviewed *at least every three years,* but any important change in your life demands immediate review. These changes might include:

- Birth, death, marriage, divorce, or disability of you or a beneficiary

- A large increase or decrease in the net worth of you or a beneficiary

- Substantial change in the type of your assets

- Purchase or sale of a business

- Change of residence to another state

- Change in tax law

What is probate?

Probate is a court proceeding to transfer title from the decedent's name to the living beneficiaries. Probate occurs in the state of your legal residence, as well as any state where you own real property.

The length of time to complete a probate varies from state to state, but can take six to eighteen months, on average. Probate is frustrating to the heirs and has the disadvantage of being public record.

Do I need a will if I have a small estate?

Everyone should have a will and/or trust. Many people believe that if there is no will, all the decedent's assets will simply be distributed to the surviving spouse. This is not always the case. If you do not create a valid will, state law dictates where your assets go and who will administer your estate.

In other words, state law may not distribute your assets to the people you want to have them. The court will also appoint someone to act as a private investigator to find family members. If you don't have a will, a determination of heirship will be required, which is a very expensive and time-consuming court proceeding.

Why shouldn't I write a will for myself?

I have never seen a will that someone prepared for themselves (with or without an online program) that accomplished *exactly* what that person intended. This means costly court proceedings are likely for your heirs. In Texas, there are two different kinds of probate: an *independent administration* is simpler, lasts only two to three months, and costs between $4000 and $6000, if everything goes smoothly.

A *dependent administration* is more complicated, can take over two years to settle, and can cost over $15,000. Most do-it-yourself wills elect this more complicated process, also costing the family over $15,000.

I had a client show me a will that his brother prepared online. The brother was mad at his children, as the children had treated him badly and hadn't spoken to him in over 15 years. He drew up his own will using a popular online program. In this will, he said, "I give my personal and business assets to my brother."

What he meant was *I give everything I own personally and in my business to my brother*. He wanted to give everything to his brother, obviously. But the only thing he owned on death was a house. The court considered his house real estate and said it was not covered by his will. The way the court defines personal property is: items you own that are not real estate.

If I have four children, shouldn't everything just be split four ways?

Most parents are concerned about being fair to all of their children. This does not, however, mean that dividing every asset evenly between them is the best thing to do.

In other cases, the children are more likely to be stressed and unable to agree on what to do with the house, or how to manage a business. It is generally kinder and more supportive to figure out how to be fair to the children *while* minimizing joint ownership or responsibilities.

Does a will cover all my assets?

Wills do not cover assets held as joint tenants (owned by two or more persons) with right of survivorship, retirement plans, annuities, life insurance, financial accounts payable on death, or transfer on death designations.

Does my out-of-state will work here?

Out-of-state wills should be reviewed by an in-state attorney. One of the things the attorney should check for is whether the will provides for an independent administration, which is the simpler and easier probate, or if it provides for a dependent administration, which is more complicated and expensive.

Does having a will avoid probate?

A will is not effective until it is legally proven in court through the probate process. I have people come to me all the time and say, "Here is Mom's will. She left everything to Dad, so Dad owns it automatically." I have to explain that until the will is admitted to probate, it does not have the legal authority of transferring title.

So how can I avoid probate?

A properly funded trust can avoid probate and save the family from having to go through the hassle of probate.

What are trusts, exactly?

A trust document is an agreement between three people dealing with assets: The *trustor* is the creator of the arrangement who appoints a *trustee* to hold the legal title to the subject assets for the benefit of the *beneficiary*.

Although there are certain legal limitations, it is possible for the trustor and beneficiary to be the same person. It is even possible for the trustor to serve as his or her own trustee. In some situations, trustors may prefer that a bank or other entity serve as the trustee.

Do I need a trust if I already have a will?

A will can be effective only after death. Because we are living much longer these days, we are more likely to become incapacitated before we die. For this reason alone, we need a way to have our affairs managed during a period of temporary or permanent incapacity as well as at the time of death.

It may also be desirable for us to set the terms for how estate assets are to be distributed. For both of these reasons, a trust is a valuable part of everyone's estate plan.

What benefits does a trust offer?

Here is why a trust (or trusts) might be a good choice for you and your family:

- Probate avoidance
- Retention of privacy regarding family assets and finances

- Avoidance of guardianship

- Creditor protection for your beneficiaries

- Control of distribution and management of assets during life and after death

Are my assets titled into the name of my trust?

Once the trust is set up, you then have to title the asset in the name of the trust. Otherwise, they are not owned by the trust. If it is in any name other than the trust, the trustee will have no legal right to distribute or manage it. The asset would likely be subject to probate just as if there were no trust.

Who controls the assets in my trust?

Most of the time it is you and your spouse. Someone else (or a trust company) will take over control if you pass away or become incompetent.

Why is funding my trust so important?

The only way a trust works as it was intended is if the assets are in the name of the trust when something goes wrong (like death or disability). The assets must be in the name of the trust to avoid court involvement.

What happens if I forget to transfer an asset?

This is why we prepare a "pour-over will" as a safety net. If an asset is left out of the trust, then the will can be probated to put that asset into the name of the trust.

What about property that does not have a title?

We prepare a "general assignment of personal property," which will cover the property you own that does not have a title.

What about out-of-state property?

It is very important that out-of-state property is transferred into the name of the trust. Otherwise, your family will be required to probate the will in more than one state, which can be very expensive.

What if I buy new assets after I fund my trust?

Those assets should be purchased in the name of the trust.

My child is married and I don't trust his spouse. How can he keep his inheritance out of her grasp, just in case they get a divorce?

Under Texas law, inheritances are the separate property of your child and not community property. His spouse has no right to the inheritance.

Of course, what your child does after he receives the inheritance can change what was once his separate property into community property. The most typical example is the child who receives the inheritance and places the assets into a joint bank account. Once he does that, it may not be his separate property anymore.

So, the best approach is to make sure he does not commingle these newly received assets with joint assets belonging to him and his spouse.

Certain types of living trusts, like a Heritage Trust, can help greatly in preserving these inherited assets as separate property.

Does a bypass trust have any disadvantages?

Bypass trusts are designed to reduce or eliminate the Federal Estate (Death) Tax that would normally be incurred upon the death of the widow or widower. Keep in mind that everything has disadvantages, including bypass trusts.

Initial cost, complexity, and maintenance costs after the first spouse dies are some of these. So, whether the bypass trust is a good choice for you or not depends upon your circumstances. A good estate planning attorney can help you decide.

Will my out-of-state health care documents work?

One of the problems with out-of-state documents is that they are not on the forms doctors in your state are used to looking at. In an emergency situation, you want the doctors to be able to act quickly.

My child just turned 18. What documents should he or she have?

There should be a HIPAA consent form that will allow the parents (and anyone else your child chooses) to receive information in the event of his or her incapacity. There should also be a health-care power of attorney. This allows the child to name who will make medical decisions for him or her.

Without these forms in place (and easily available to doctors and health care providers), parents could learn that their child has been in an accident, but no one would be able to tell them about their child's condition. If the child is in a coma for an extended period of time and can't give the appropriate consent, the parents might have to go to court to obtain guardianship in order to get information or participate in treatment decisions for their child.

There should also be a directive to physicians in which the child gives instructions regarding if and when life support measures should be employed, as well as when they should not.

These are big decisions for anyone, but necessary for the benefit of young adults and their parents. An estate planning attorney can help you create well-crafted documents that will reflect your adult child's wishes.

I create and provide an emergency document card for all my clients. It gives doctors quick access to the health care documents they need, as well as information on whom to contact.

It is something you hope you will never need. But you can rest easier knowing you can be there for your child if a medical crisis should occur.

Appendix XIV

3 Stages of Alzheimer's Every Caregiver Should Know

I have had the pleasure of working with countless Alzheimer's caregivers during my career as an elder law and estate planning attorney. And without fail, the one piece of information they want the most is the ability to understand how the disease progresses. Why? Because it helps them cope with the present and be better prepared for the future.

For that reason, I thought it would be good to outline three stages of Alzheimer's disease every caregiver should know — whether you are starting your caregiving journey, or you've been on this path for several years and are learning as you go.

3 Stages of Alzheimer's every caregiver should know

Currently, the Alzheimer's Association website lists and describes three stages of Alzheimer's.

Early Stage — Mild Alzheimer's

In the earliest stage of Alzheimer's, most people are still leading an active and independent lifestyle. They drive, go to work, take care of their children, and even take part in social activities. They don't feel that different, other than what can best be described as occasional memory lapses or difficulties that even friends and family start to notice.

Common difficulties during this stage include:

- Problems coming up with the right word or name
- Challenges with performing tasks in social or work settings
- Losing or misplacing a valuable object
- Increased difficulty with planning or organizing
- Trouble remembering names when introduced to new people

Middle Stage — Moderate Alzheimer's

This stage is typically the longest and can last for many years. As the disease progresses, dementia symptoms are much more pronounced, and the person with Alzheimer's will require a greater level of care. A person may have great difficulty performing tasks, such as paying bills, but they may still remember significant details about their life. You will eventually notice them begin to confuse words, get frustrated or angry, and even act in unexpected ways.

Common symptoms that are noticeable to everyone during this stage include:

- Forgetfulness of events or about one's own personal history
- Feeling moody or withdrawn, especially in socially or mentally challenging situations

- Confusion about where they are or what day it is
- Changes in sleep patterns and increased risk of wandering or becoming lost
- Personality and behavioral changes, including suspiciousness and delusions or repetitive behavior

Late Stage — Severe Alzheimer's

This is the final and most overwhelming stage for the person with the diagnosis and their caregivers. Individuals lose the ability to respond to their environment, carry on conversations, and control movement. Communicating pain also becomes difficult. As memory and cognitive skills worsen, significant personality changes may take place, and individuals will need extensive help with daily activities we all take for granted. This can include:

- Losing awareness of recent experiences and their surroundings
- Needing around-the-clock assistance with daily activities and personal care
- Increased difficulty communicating
- Vulnerability to infections such as pneumonia

Appendix XIV

11 Signs of Caregiver Stress and How to Combat them

If you are an Alzheimer's caregiver, then you know more than anyone how easy it can be to focus so much on your loved one's needs that you forget about caring for yourself. It may seem selfish to think of yourself in the face of such a dreaded disease someone else is facing, which is why you avoid it. But your health is an important piece to remember as you move forward in your new role — especially when it comes to combatting caregiver stress.

Not sure if you are experiencing stress? The Alzheimer's Association and Mabel Lopez, Ph.D., of the Mind and Brain Care in Fort Meyers, Florida, have come up with 11 signs of caregiver stress you may not be recognizing:

1. Denial — You may not be willing to accept that this disease is real and the effect it is having on your loved one.

2. Anger — You are finding that you are easily angered by the person with Alzheimer's, especially over the fact that they can no longer do the things they used to be able to do with ease.

3. Social withdrawal — You are slowly separating yourself from friends or activities that used to make you feel good.

4. Anxiety —You are stressing about the future and what each day will bring moving forward.

5. Depression — You no longer care. Your spirit is slowly breaking, and you are struggling to cope.

6. Exhaustion — You are beginning to find it nearly impossible to complete daily tasks.

7. Sleeplessness — You want to sleep, but you are too busy worrying about your never-ending to-do list.

8. Irritability — You just want to be left alone. Your sunny disposition has been replaced by moodiness.

9. Lack of concentration — You are finding it difficult to perform familiar tasks.

10. New or worsening health problems — Your health is becoming a bigger problem than you realized.

11. Trouble concentrating — You can't focus on anything, even something as simple as reading or watching TV.

Combatting Stress — It's all about being proactive

You will undoubtedly find yourself vulnerable to caregiver stress. This is normal. However, the best way to combat caregiver stress is to proactively avoid or minimize the potential mental and physical health risks it can cause.

Here are some tips to keep in mind:

Learn to relax

Consider breathing techniques, muscle relaxation, and positive visualization. This step doesn't come easy for many of us, so don't be afraid to reach out to a licensed counselor for help.

Ask for help

More importantly, accept help when it is offered. Don't forget that you are helping those who care about you by letting them know what they can do for you.

Recognize strength in numbers

Surround yourself with good people who have been in your shoes before. There are support groups for caregivers; attend those meetings. Doing so will help you realize you are not alone in this fight.

Take care of yourself

Don't ignore your health. Keep up with regular doctor visits and talk openly about the stresses you are experiencing through-out the caregiver journey.

Be active

Don't forget to get regular exercise, which will help you improve your physical and mental health.

If you are experiencing caregiver stress, just remember that you are not alone. However, it is up to you to get the help you need to minimize the physical and mental health risks that might result from a lack of attention to your needs.

Appendix XV

The SECURE Act: How to offset the tax consequences and protect your family

There's been quite a bit of buzz in the news recently about the Setting Every Community Up for Retirement Enhancement (SECURE) Act that was just signed by President Donald Trump. Specifically, our clients are hearing that it could negatively affect them and their retirement plans, Retirement Plan Trust, and IRA Inheritance TrustsTM.

There's a lot to unpack here, but we want to assure you that while this bill changes how retirement accounts are taxed and affects required minimum distributions, it's not all bad. And there are still ways to protect everything you own and love.

Before I get into specifics on what has changed, the most important piece of advice I can give you regarding the SECURE Act is to talk to a financial advisor so that he or she can help mitigate the tax consequences of the new law. The second most important piece of advice I can give is to talk to our office about updating your estate plan to make sure your loved ones are protected from the tax consequences of this act.

Nothing we say moving forward will help or make sense until you implement the two steps above. We will always look out for your best interests regarding any law changes. And that includes helping you find a qualified financial advisor. If you meet with your current advisor, and he or she responds with, "There's nothing to look at regarding the SECURE Act and your retirement accounts," then you need to be meeting with someone else. We are happy to recommend financial advisors whom we regularly work with for our own investments and those of our clients. Each of them understands how to protect you and your family from the consequences of this law.

For estate planning, our focus is on getting to know your family and discussing protections you want in place for the people you are leaving money to. At Leigh Hilton, PLLC, we have helped over 6,000 families protect the assets that they leave to their loved ones from divorce, creditors, and lawsuits. We've also helped over 300 families implement the plans that we've designed. And the reason that's important to you is because when you put together a plan, what's important to you is that it works on the back end. The planning we do will also need to be customized to your beneficiaries' actual situations.

Now that we've got that out of the way, let's discuss the reasons for the SECURE Act and its major talking points.

What has changed under the SECURE Act?

The reality is that not a lot of Americans are prepared for retirement. The SECURE Act is the largest piece of retirement legislation in a long time and includes significant provisions designed to give more access to tax-advantaged accounts while also preventing older Americans from outliving their assets. The bill also adjusts long-standing rules related to tax-advantaged retirement accounts. Here are just a few of the changes that stand out:

- The age for required minimum distributions (RMDs) has been pushed back from 70 1/2 to 72.

- Because of the age change to 72, you have more time to do Roth IRA conversions.

- Many older individuals will now have the ability to contribute to tax-deductible IRAs after 70 1/2 and save for the future.

- Retirement plans for small-business owners who want them for employees are less expensive and easier to manage.

- Many part-time workers are now eligible for employer retirement plans.

- The bill expands what 529 college savings accounts may be used for, allowing for more flexibility.

Comparison of the Old Law and the SECURE Act, and the removal of the "stretch" provision

The biggest talking point is that the SECURE Act has removed the "stretch" provision for beneficiaries of IRAs and things like 401(k)s. Under the Old Law, the beneficiary could stretch out the RMDs over his or her own lifetime, which could be a very long time if the beneficiary was significantly younger. Naturally, most of our clients liked the idea of being able to have their retirement plans last for the entirety of their children's or grandchildren's lifetime. Those with larger retirement plan savings also liked being able to protect their beneficiaries from losing the money to divorce, creditors, or lawsuits. Also, my clients who are grandparents wanted to make sure that their retirement accounts made it to the grandchildren.

Under the new law, if you die, your heirs might have to do a full distribution within 10 years of your death.

There are several exceptions to that:
- A surviving spouse may use their own life expectancy.

- Children of the retirement plan owner who are under the age of majority can take minimum distributions until they reach the age of majority. After that, it is a 10-year payout. The age of majority is the age of majority in the state the person with the retirement plan lived in at the time of his death. In Texas and 46 other states, the age is 18. In Mississippi, it is 21.

- A person who is disabled. Disabled is defined as being unable to be substantially employed, which is the same standard used for Social Security disability benefits. Being substantially unable to be employed means you cannot make a living. It's not that you're unemployed, it's that you're unemployable — meaning you cannot work.

- Chronically ill individuals.

- An individual not more than 10 years younger than the person who owned the retirement plan.

Anyone who had a loved one pass away prior to December 31, 2019, will still be subject to the old rules of minimum distribution. If you have someone who died last year, and it hasn't been more than nine months, meet with us to look at maybe passing it down to the children or grandchildren to continue maximizing the available stretch. If you had a loved one pass away prior to December 31, 2019, and you're already taking minimum distributions, you can continue to take the minimum distributions over their life expectancy under the old rules.

Comparisons of the Old Law and the SECURE Act, and the consequences on growth

The changes to the "stretch" provision bring forth several significant consequences in terms of growth. For example, let's assume you are leaving $500,000 in retirement accounts to a beneficiary who is 40 years old, and the money is growing at 6% before taxes and 4.75% after taxes, and the beneficiary is in a 24% tax bracket. If the beneficiary takes 10 equal distributions, the money will have grown to $2,582,651.00 when that beneficiary reaches age 79. Under the Old Law, if the same assumptions applied, the beneficiary would be able to draw from the retirement account over his life expectancy. And in that case, the money will have grown to $3,251,331.00. The difference is almost a million dollars.

One thing that hasn't changed, and should be avoided, occurs when the retirement plan is made payable to a living trust that does not meet the rules to be a designated beneficiary. The resulting distributions are then subject to a 5-year payout. This allows less opportunity for growth and faster taxation of the money.

Future adjustments to estate planning

I mentioned earlier that there are still ways to protect everything you own and everyone you love. With traditional retirement plans, if you put money in without paying tax on it, somebody is going to have to pay tax on it when it's pulled out. Mathematically, we might want to do something different than what you're currently doing so that whoever pulls from your retirement account gets the most advantages possible. The assumption most people make is that they are going to be in a lower tax bracket when they retire. The current tax rates for the higher wage earners are lower under the current tax law. Have your financial advisor run the numbers based on the current tax rates and what rates are projected to be in the future.

Also, if you are married, the amount of income you can earn at the lower tax brackets is twice what it would be if your spouse passes away and you are filing as a single person. That is one of the things your financial advisor can analyze and should analyze when looking at a Roth conversion.

Will there be law changes in the future, and how do we adjust for them?

Trusts that are drafted by our office have trust protector language that allows us to make changes as the law changes. Specifically, we have language in our documents that says we can make adjustments for new laws even after you pass away or become incompetent. That means we can go in and modify the language to say whatever we need it to say to comply with the current laws. Doing so gives you the most flexibility on how to adjust for the new law.

My guess is that this law is the first of many sweeping changes to how retirement plans are taxed. Congress has talked for years about taxing people for having too much in retirement. That is why it is important to work with an attorney and financial planner who keeps up with the changes in law and can design your plan to adjust for those changes.

Our law firm belongs to many professional organizations that are looking at this new law, and we're making sure that we draft the best possible language to adjust for the new law and for any other laws that come along. These groups include over 3,000 attorneys nationwide. I also subscribe to many newsletters and have listened to education programs by CPAs and financial advisors who are nationally known experts in retirement plans and taxation.

If I have a Retirement Plan Trust or IRA Inheritance Trust™, do I need to make any changes?

In analyzing what changes, if any, need to be made to your Retirement Plan Trust or IRA Inheritance TrustTM, we will start with looking at how responsible your beneficiaries are. When looking at this, we will need to know about the actual ability of these beneficiaries to handle money — not how you wish they would handle their finances, or the more mature behavior you anticipate in the future.

The reason our clients set up a Retirement Plan Trust is to protect their retirement plans if the beneficiaries get divorced, if they get sued, or they have creditor or predator problems. We can also assure that the retirement plan stays in the family. So, if you want it to go to your kids and then grandkids, we can design a plan that makes that happen.

If you have someone you're leaving money to who is responsible and can handle inheriting the money, their getting it out over a 10-year period is not going to be that big of a deal. With that said, it is still worth talking to a financial advisor about managing the tax consequences of them getting the money over a 10-year period instead of over their life expectancy. The beneficiaries are going to be taxed a little bit faster, and they might be taxed at a higher rate. We will also want to discuss protecting the retirement account from divorce, creditors, and lawsuits, as well as keeping it in the family.

If you have someone who is irresponsible, leaving them too much too quickly could ruin their lives. In those situations, we need to discuss putting protections in place so that the beneficiary doesn't receive the money too quickly. We should also discuss ways to reduce the tax consequences of that decision. The most important thing to focus on is what you are wanting to accomplish and not letting the tax tail wag the dog.

One of the common mistakes people make is focusing on only taxes and not the results they actually wish to accomplish. It would be better to pay a little more in taxes and have the funds protected. For example, if you leave a large retirement plan to a person in his 20s, is he still going to have an incentive to be gainfully employed or to get an education? Most inheritances end up being treated exactly like lottery winnings, meaning they are blown within one year. The number one answer to what someone is going to do after winning the lottery is quit their job. The number two answer is they are going to spend every dime.

If you take a 20-year-old who's currently in college or working their first job, is he or she going to continue to work if there is $100,000 a year coming in for the next 10 years? So it's a conversation of, do we want to keep it inside the trust instead of having it paid out with the accompanying tax consequences? Tax rates on income retained inside of a trust are higher than if they are distributed to the beneficiary. These tax consequences can be offset by planning with a good financial advisor.

Wouldn't it be better to pay a little more in taxes and have your beneficiary finish college and stay gainfully employed so that he or she can grow in responsibility and advance to a better job in the future?

What if my financial advisor says the SECURE Act is no big deal, and no analysis is needed?

In this case, as we said at the beginning of this book, you need a new financial advisor. I would be concerned if my financial advisor was not keeping up with new laws. I would love to introduce you to a financial advisor who is proactive in saving taxes and keeping up with new laws.

In January, I was told by two different financial advisors that they had heard there was a new law but hadn't had time to look at anything on it. One large investing firm sent a memo to its financial advisors saying the SECURE Act is a law, and that only attorneys should be giving advice on it. In reality, the new law is full of financial planning opportunities, and your financial advisor should be on top of these and prepared to offer them to you. If you have a financial advisor whom you love working with, I would be happy to meet with him or her to discuss the SECURE Act. I have spoken with several about what I think they need to emphasize to their clients. I can show the financial advisor ways to save taxes.

Why do I need a Retirement Plan Trust?

When you're trying to think through the people you're leaving money to, see if any of these possibilities may apply:

- The wrong people eventually inheriting the assets. For example, if you leave money to your daughter, and she passes away, most likely she's going to leave everything to her husband. And if he passes away, he will probably leave everything to his next wife, an outcome that could disinherit the grandkids. So, if we leave money directly to people and don't have it inside of a trust, we can't control where it goes next. Some of my clients actually like the son-in-law or the daughter-in-law enough to want them taken care of, but still want to make sure it goes to the grandkids after the son-in-law or daughter-in-law's death.

- Poor spending habits of the beneficiaries, their spouses, or children. Your loved ones can be influenced by their family to spend the money. Most of my clients are bothered by the fact that what they have worked all their lives to accumulate is probably going to be spent within one year.

- Do your beneficiaries have the money management skills to handle the amount they are inheriting? They might be really good with the money they have, but they may not be able to manage what they're being given. What a lot of our clients do is have the beneficiary use the clients' current financial advisor because they have been using this person and know they will be able to properly manage the money for the beneficiary.

- The beneficiary's spouse could take some of your retirement accounts in a divorce if you give it to the beneficiary outright.

- If they're young, elderly, or disabled, they may not be able to manage the money that you're leaving them.

- If they're on government benefits, any sort of disability, and on needs-based government benefits, anything over $2,000 will throw them off. And even though we have the Affordable Care Act, that doesn't mean most people can get health insurance. The problem is that you must be employed for the Affordable Care Act to apply. So, if someone is born with a disability and needs to be on Medicaid to have health insurance, and you leave them more than $2,000 outright, you can throw them off of Medicaid. Instead, you can leave money in a Special Needs Trust and not mess up Medicaid eligibility.

- If the retirement is left outright to the beneficiary, lawsuits, creditors, or even bankruptcy can grab the retirement account.

- Estate tax when they pass it down. The current estate tax exemption is over $11 million. Most of us don't have enough to worry about that now. But the exemption amount that matters as far as the estate taxes are concerned is the exemption in the year you pass away. The odds are high that during our lifetime, they will reduce the amount of the exemption. And the odds are even higher that the exemption amount will be reduced during your beneficiaries' lifetimes. The federal government taxes everything over the exemption at approximately 47%.

Case Study

As we approach the end of our discussion, I want to walk you through a brief case study.

Bob is married to Betty. On Bob's retirement plans, Betty is the primary beneficiary, and then it's going to be the kids. They have three children. Bob Jr. has got a high-maintenance wife, is in a business where he's likely to get sued, and because he is successful, there's going to be a second estate tax when the money's paid down. If the parents leave the retirement account to him outright, the money is vulnerable to those three things.

Jane is the middle child. She has a problem marriage. Actually, her parents have more of a problem with her marriage than she does. They just really don't like or trust who she's married to. So they're thinking in the event that she dies, they don't want him to inherit money. Or, if they ever get divorced, they don't want him to take any of it. Jane also lacks the ability to manage the money. So, the protection I recommend is requiring Jane to use Bob and Betty's financial advisor to make sure that she has somebody professional to help her take care of the money.

And then there are some families who have a Joe. Joe is the one who never quite gets it right. Joe has had to file for bankruptcy a couple of times and might qualify for government benefits but has never gotten diagnosed. So Joe needs to be protected against himself. Joe is also very soft-hearted, and if he ever has more than he actually needs for the near future, he will give it away. He is not looking at his long-term needs.

In doing an estate plan for Bob and Betty, we are going to look at protecting the money they leave to their children from third parties or the federal government. We would recommend a Retirement Plan Trust. The spouse is usually the beneficiary. Under the SECURE Act, we are going to look at passing part of the retirement accounts on the first spouse's death down to the children and grandchildren to allow two different 10-year periods for distribution. We will, of course, also need to analyze whether the surviving spouse will have enough money to last their lifetime.

We occasionally will put the retirement accounts in the Retirement Plan Trust on the first death if the surviving spouse is starting to have trouble, has been diagnosed with Alzheimer's or dementia, or is starting to make bad financial decisions. We might also put the retirement accounts in the trust on the first death if we want to make sure the surviving spouse leaves it the way the two spouses have agreed, and doesn't leave it to whomever they marry.

We would recommend that Bob Jr.'s portion be left to him in the trust. We can allow him to be in charge, but the money is protected if he gets divorced or sued, and we can protect it against a second estate tax.

And we would recommend the same thing for Jane. We would recommend that the trust require her to use a financial planner. If she's really bad with money, and we think she can't handle managing it, then we put somebody else in charge.

Should we put Joe in charge? I'm amazed at the number of families that I have to talk out of putting Joe in charge. The logic is that if you put Bob in charge and put Jane in charge, it's only fair to Joe that he gets to be in charge. The parents are usually concerned that it will hurt his feelings if you don't let him be in charge. But if you think about it, at this stage, you've probably been protecting Joe for a good portion of his life. So why would you stop now? And really, putting him in charge is probably going to totally mess up how he does things. The other dynamic that I find quite frequently is when we have one person in a couple who clearly wants to protect Joe forever, while the other parent says it's his problem and that we're done raising him.

In this case, we would create three different sub-trusts — one for each child with different terms for each. It is still important to have a Retirement Plan Trust to protect the money over the 10 years and beyond.

Roth IRAs allow us to protect the retirement accounts beyond the 10 years and have the protections against losing the money to divorce, creditors, and lawsuits over the beneficiary's lifetime without tax consequences. There are additional options that should be explored with

a financial advisor for protection over a lifetime and for reducing taxes.

Managing the income tax consequences of that 10-year rule

Even under the new law, you will want to take advantage of money growing over time. The rule of 72 enables us to calculate how long it takes for money to double at different interest rates. It is calculated by dividing the interest rate into 72. At 6%, money doubles every 12 years. If we can have it where the money grows throughout your lifetime and the beneficiaries' lifetime, we have many opportunities for this money to double. Most of my clients like the idea of the money lasting over their children or grandchildren's lifetimes and being protected against the outside world. We can still do that; we just need to manage some of the tax consequences related to the SECURE Act.

Here are some key concepts as far as figuring out what to do. We want to retain income tax deferral — meaning we want to pay as little as possible in tax. We might be biting the bullet and paying the tax now rather than when you pass away — the goal is to pay as little in taxes as possible in the long run.

The other thing to look at is the bracket management within the family. You might want to strategically shift the Retirement Plan Trust to say that there's more than one beneficiary — especially if under the Old Law you wanted this money to benefit your kids, and then your grandkids. And, of course, you thought that was going to be sequentially. We now will talk about doing it at the same time. One of the ways we can manage income tax brackets is to distribute the income to as many people as possible to get it on as many tax returns as possible and focus on getting it to people with lower tax rates. For example, if you were to leave the retirement plan to six different kids, grandkids, nieces, and nephews, the tax rates will be lower because the money is going to be spread out to more beneficiaries. But the primary focus needs to be on whom you want to leave money to — not just taxes.

In calculating how much to convert to a Roth IRA, one of the calculations needs to be what tax bracket are you in? The amount would be determined by how much more income you could have before entering the next bracket.

We should also look at whether you are charitably inclined. If you are leaving money to a charity, this is the best money to leave them because charities don't pay income tax. Also, it is worth discussing getting a tax deduction now for committing to give money to a charity when you pass away. Some of my clients give their retirement plans to charity and replace the amount their children would have received with life insurance, because the life insurance will go to the children tax-free. You can also have the children receive income for life. If you're interested in that, we can run an illustration to see if it makes sense for your family.

The other really important thing is, if you're taking minimum distributions, and you're giving to a charity the same amount of money, it's better to make the minimum distributions go directly to the charity. There's a tax advantage to doing that. Have your financial advisor look into it.

The other thing to have financial advisors discuss with you is whether life insurance makes sense to offset the tax consequences of the new law. So what we might do is have the insurance replace the amount that's going to have to go to tax. This enables your kids and grandkids or nieces and nephews to receive the amount they would have received under the Old Law. And these are all things that can be determined with a mathematical calculation.

Summary

In conclusion, I would highly recommend that you discuss this new law with your financial advisor and CPA, and that you attend one of our upcoming seminars on the SECURE Act. You can see the schedule for upcoming seminars on our website, https://dentonestateplanninglawyer.com/secure-act-changes-seminar-2020/.

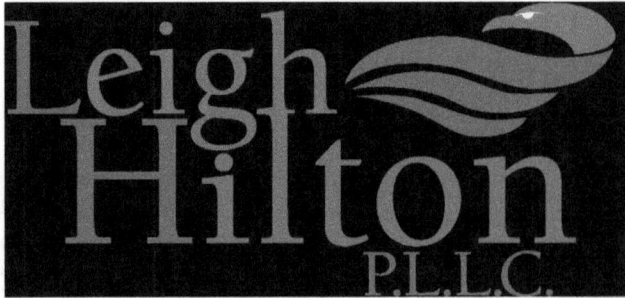

For Information contact:

940.387.8800

918 N. Elm Suite 100 • Denton, TX 76201

401 S Main St • Aubrey, TX 76227

124 McMakin Rd • Bartonville, TX 76226

www.DentonEstatePlanningLawyer.com